Skills for **Employability**

Step UP

Coursebook and **eBook**

A2+

Linda Butler
Robyn Brinks Lockwood
Amy Renehan
Jenni Currie Santamaria

Step Up A2+

Pearson Education, 221 River Street, Hoboken, NJ 07030 USA

Cover Illustration: Roy Hermelin

Text composition: Straive

Library of Congress Cataloging-in-Publication Data: A catalog record for the print edition is available from the Library of Congress.

Printed in the United States of America

ISBN-13: 978-0-13-747351-9

1 2022

pearsonenglish.com/stepup

Acknowledgments

We would like to thank the following people for their help with this project.

Güzide Göksen Birol, Istanbul Okan University; **Eduardo Pinell Campuzano,** CIU Director, Universidad Privada Franz Tamayo; **Meg Cassamally,** University of Siena; **Adrian Crawley,** Evority Learning Centre; University of Siena; **Yabancı Diller,** School of Foreign Languages; **Louise Dixon,** Director of Studies at Hallo! Servizi Linguistici; **Aybala Eren,** Gazi University; **Alex Fayle,** Well & Will Language Academy; **Elizabeth Cruz Flores,** Tecnológico de Monterrey; **Jacques Friggieri,** Redrob; **María Amparo Garcia,** ICPNA Cusco; **Christina Gebbia,** Director of Let's Talk English Center in Valencia; **Maria de la Paz Giglio,** New Concept School of English; **Zeynep Güler,** İstanbul Okan University; **Ilaria Incorvaia,** ITIS 'Antonio Meucci', Florence; **Nancy Johnstone,** School of Engineering, UBA, Buenos Aires, Argentina; **Sevil Altıkulaçoğlu Kayaer,** Gazi University; **Yeliz Korkmaz,** Yıldız Technical University, Turkey; **Héctor Raúl Sánchez Lozano,** Proulex Universidad de Guadalajara; **Mariana Juana Aviles Martillo,** coordinator of CEFI, Center for Continuing Educatiòn and Interamerican Labor; **Anne Marie Mc Gowan,** University of Rome ' Tor Vergata ' Italy; **Cristian Meléndez,** Universidad Católica de El Salvador; **Jose Manuel Mendivil S.,** Centro Boliviano Americano - Fundación Cultural y Educativa La Paz; **Paul Cruz Montenegro,** English Coordinator of CRC - Peru Cruceros; **M.Àngels Nogué,** Centre D'Idiomes Olot; **Irem Ozcan,** Gazi University, College of Foreign Languages; **Claudia Posarelli,** ITIS Meucci Firenze; **Steven Pragnell,** Astex Servicios Lingüísticos, Madrid; **María de Lourdes Camarillo Rodríguez,** Escuela Bancaria y Comercial; **Raquel Sánchez,** Faculty of Education in Albacete (UCLM); **Chayapak Tangapiwut,** Burapha University Language Institute; **Onur Uludag,** Yildiz Technical University; **Taku Umeda,** Tokyo Business and Language College; **Laura Vacca**, Inglese su Misura; **Marijke van Leuven,** Oxford School of English, Verona, Italy.

Photo Credits Page 2: Shutterstock; Page 5 (top): Rawpixel/123RF; 5 (bottom): Nattakorn Maneerat/123RF; 6: Ammentorp/123RF; 6 (mobile icons): Ico Maker/Shutterstock; 6 (thumbs up emoji): Flower travelin man/Shutterstock; 6 (money bag emoji): Vladwel/Shutterstock; 6 (angry emoji): SpicyTruffel/Shutterstock; 8: Alekup/123RF; Page 9: ESB Professional/Shutterstock; 10: Ammentorp/123RF; 11: Theshots/123RF; Page 13: Marek CECH/Shutterstock; 14: Dinis Tolipov/123RF; 15 (top): Prostock-studio/Shutterstock; 15 (center): Vadym Drobot/123RF; 15 (bottom): Vadym Drobot/123RF; 16 (enjoy life icon): NartGraphic/Shutterstock; 16 (exercise icon): Pking4th/Shutterstock; 16 (improve diet icon): Pking4th/Shutterstock; 16 (save money icon): VitaminCo/Shutterstock; 16 (get organized icon): Pking4th/Shutterstock; 16 (family time icon): Lara Cold/Shutterstock; 16 (hobby and skill icon): Yindee/Shutterstock; 16 (quit smoking icon): Pking4th/Shutterstock; 16 (reading icon): Incomible/Shutterstock; Page 17: GuruXOX/Shutterstock; 19 (volunteers): Syda Productions/Shutterstock; 19 (woman): Ferli/123RF; 19 (mobile icons): Ico Maker/Shutterstock; 19 (man): Wavebreak Media Ltd/123RF; 20 (bees): Jacek Nowak/123RF; 20 (wolves): Alexander Sviridov/Shutterstock; 20 (geese): Gino Santa Maria/123RF; Page 21: ImageFlow/Shutterstock; 22: I. Pilon/Shutterstock; 23 (traffic light): Shotmedia/Shutterstock; 23 (brownstones): Sneaky Buddy/Shutterstock; 23 (stop sign): Christian Delbert/Shutterstock; 23 (office): Zhu difeng/Shutterstock; Page 25: Fizkes/Shutterstock; 26 (top): GaudiLab/Shutterstock; 26 (center): Shutterstock; 26 (bottom): LDprod/Shutterstock; 27: Michaeljung/Shutterstock; 28 (Ghandi): New creative ideas/Shutterstock; 28 (Mandela): Alessia Pierdomenico/Shutterstock; 28 (Alexander): Andreas Wolochow/Shutterstock; 28 (Cleopatra): Konstantin Yolshin/Shutterstock; Page 29: Pathdoc/Shutterstock; 30: El Nariz/Shutterstock; 31 (top): Dolgachov/123RF; 31 (bottom): ALPA PROD/Shutterstock; 32: Pixel Embargo/Shutterstock; Page 33: Ground Picture/Shutterstock; 34 (doctor): PhotoBankIndia/Shutterstock; 34 (stressed student): Tom Wang/Shutterstock; 34 (runner): Rido/Shutterstock; 35: New Africa/Shutterstock; 36 (apple): Ianlusung/Shutterstock; 36 (watch): VasutinSergey/Shutterstock; 36 (jogger): Ellegant/Shutterstock; 36 (speech bubble): James weston/Shutterstock; 36 (heart): Djordje Radivojevic/Shutterstock; 36 (coffee): JATUTAPE NONTAWIRAT/Shutterstock; Page 37 (top left): Shutterstock; 37 (top right): Vadym Pastukh/Shutterstock; 37 (bottom left): XiXinXing/Shutterstock; 37 (bottom right): BGStock72/Shutterstock; 40 (French flag): Ahmad Muflih Syarifuddin/Shutterstock; 40 (Japanese flag): Ahmad Muflih Syarifuddin/Shutterstock; 40 (Swedish flag): Ahmad Muflih Syarifuddin/Shutterstock; 40 (Egyptian flag): Ahmad Muflih Syarifuddin/Shutterstock; Page 41: Shutter_M/Shutterstock; 42: Roquillo Tebar/Shutterstock; 43 (Lucia Martinez): Roquillo Tebar/Shutterstock; 43 (boats): Balate Dorin/Shutterstock; 43 (panda): Photo by Lola/Shutterstock; 43 (seafood market): Natnatnat/Shutterstock; 43 (profile avatar): Atstock Productions/Shutterstock; 43 (sofa): Laschon Maximilian/123RF; 43 (table): Lynnette/Shutterstock; 43 (dining chairs): Betelejze/Shutterstock; 44 (woman): PureSolution/Shutterstock; 44 (man): PureSolution/Shutterstock; Page 45: Shutterstock; 46: El Nariz/Shutterstock; 47 (top): Seventyfour74/123RF; 47 (bottom): Shutterstock; Page 49: Fizkes/Shutterstock; 50 (top): Ambrophoto/Shutterstock; 50 (bottom): Metamorworks/Shutterstock; 51: Ana Blazic Pavlovic/123RF; 52 (left): Fizkes/123RF; 52 (center): Cast Of Thousands/Shutterstock; 52 (right): Estam/Shutterstock; 52 (right, image advert): Asier Romero/Shutterstock; Page 72 (avatar): Gurza/Shutterstock; 73 (avatars): Gurza/Shutterstock; 74 (avatar): Gurza/Shutterstock; 77 (avatar): Gurza/Shutterstock; 78 (avatars): Gurza/Shutterstock; 79 (health icons): Tulpahn/Shutterstock; 80 (avatar): Gurza/Shutterstock; 82 (avatars): Gurza/Shutterstock; 83 (avatar): Gurza/Shutterstock.

Scope and Sequence

Welcome page 2	In the classroom | Learn about your book | Meet Your Employability Skills Coaches

Module	I can . . .	Learning Objectives	Vocabulary
1 **Communication 1** How to Communicate Successfully pages 5–8	I can identify successful communication skills.	• Identify ways to communicate a message effectively • Decide the best way to communicate with my audience • Decide the best medium to use for communicating a message • Identify ways to deliver a clear message	*accurate, affect, breakdown, detail, facial expression, formal, informal, interfere, impression, preference, react, record*
2 **Communication 2** Effective Communication at Work pages 9–12	I can identify effective oral communication skills in the workplace.	• Identify good listening skills • Describe how to manage emotions • Identify effective messaging • Describe effective body language	*blame, calm down, confirm, emotion, express, interrupt, involved, neutral, misunderstanding, pay attention, respond, upset*
3 **Goal Setting** SMART Goals pages 13–16	I can explain the importance of setting SMART goals and describe how to create them.	• Describe SMART goals • Explain the importance of setting goals • State how to improve a SMART goal	*actually, concentrate, detailed, directly, exactly, figure out, on average, original, positive, realistic, related, set aside, side effect, time frame*
4 **Teamwork** Being a Team Player pages 17–20	I can explain the importance of teamwork and describe the skills of an effective team.	• Describe the benefits of working on a team • Describe teamwork skills • State how to improve teamwork skills	*active role, conflict, encourage, flexible, get along with, opinion, rely on, responsible, strength, solve, supportive, weakness*
5 **Critical Thinking** Critical Thinking Skills pages 21–24	I can explain and describe the steps in the critical thinking process.	• Define critical thinking • Describe the steps in the critical thinking process • Identify ways to improve critical thinking	*analyze, claim, decision, dishonest, evaluate, evidence, identify, issue, respected, review, source, viewpoint*
6 **Leadership** Leadership Skills pages 25–28	I can describe the skills needed to lead people effectively.	• Describe the qualities of a good leader • Explain the importance of leadership skills • Identify ways to improve leadership skills	*attitude, brave, feedback, innovation, inspire, motivate, opportunity, outgoing, quality, respect, responsibility, value*

Pronunciation	Language Strategy	Project	Talk!
The sound /ʃ/	Listen for examples	Analyze communication skills in different situations	Facts about communication problems at work
The sound /ər/	Listen for reasons	Interview people about their communication skills	Annoying habits of co-workers
Silent letters	Listen for sequencing words	Share your SMART goals	New Year's resolutions survey
Stressed syllables	Listen for enumeration	Survey people about their experiences working in teams	How animals live and work in teams
The letter *a*	Take notes on critical thinking	Evaluate an issue and come up with a plan	The importance of critical skills in the workplace
The letter *o*	Listen for introductory phrases	Research a famous leader	Imagine you are the leader of a new country

Module	I can . . .	Learning Objectives	Vocabulary
7 **Self-Management** Time Management pages 29–32	I can describe specific strategies for managing and planning my time.	• Describe the benefits of using time management tools • Describe four specific time management tools • Identify effective time management strategies	*assignment, catch up, category, deadline, organized, overwhelmed, pile up, put off, rank, strategy, stressful, workload*
8 **Wellness** Healthy Habits pages 33–36	I can identify healthy and unhealthy habits.	• Identify healthy and unhealthy habits • Describe the benefits of having healthy habits • Describe the effects of unhealthy habits	*active, blood pressure, carbohydrate, diabetes, fiber, injury, lactose, lean, mental, muscle, physical, protein, poultry*
9 **Social Responsibility** Personal Responsibility pages 37–40	I can explain the importance of personal social responsibility and describe workplace etiquette.	• Define social responsibility • Explain personal responsibility • Describe workplace etiquette • Identify ways to improve workplace etiquette	*adjust, appropriately, atmosphere, disrespect, distract, focus, negative, productive, promotion, rude, signal, tone*
10 **Branding** Branding Basics pages 41–44	I can describe strategies for building my personal brand.	• Define what a personal brand is • Describe specific strategies for building a personal brand • Identify effective mission statements	*achieve, creative, description, emphasize, highlight, impress, match, notice, ongoing, personality, reflect, revise*
11 **Job Search** What Is Networking? pages 45–48	I can describe specific strategies for building and growing my professional network.	• Define what a professional network is • Explain the benefits of networking • Describe specific strategies for building and growing a professional network	*advice, effective, establish, expand, get-together, in touch with, purpose, reach out, relate, separately, training, update*
12 **Interviewing** Interview Basics pages 49–52	I can describe specific strategies for preparing for a job interview.	• Explain the importance of preparing for a job interview • Describe specific strategies for preparing for a job interview	*a good fit, applicant, casual, confident, discussion, document, dress code, duty, neat, professional, requirement, reference, values*

Check your understanding ....page 54
Discussion strategies...................page 68
Vocabulary practice ....page 72
Glossary ....page 86

Pronunciation	Language Strategy	Project	Talk!
Dropped syllables	Keep your notes short	Choose an appropriate planning tool for an event	Discuss different planning tools
The vowels /i/ and /ɪ/	Identify cause and effect	Research a health app or website	How to create good habits
The vowel /ə/ in unstressed syllables	Leave space and adding information later	Research more tips and examples of good and bad workplace etiquette	Workplace culture in different countries
The voiced *th* sound /ð/	Identify definitions	Write your mission statement	How important is personal branding
The vowel sound /^/	Ask and answer questions	Research two professional groups	Discuss survey results about jobs and networks
Consonant groups	Make inferences	Research a company	Discuss unusual things people did to get a job

To the Teacher

Overview

Step Up is a flexible online course designed for adults or young adults who want to improve their employability skills—whether to get a first job, secure a promotion, find a different job, re-enter the workforce after an absence, or change fields. Although the emphasis of the course is on employability skills, *Step Up* also develops English language skills by providing vocabulary instruction and practice, listening, reading, and notetaking skills, pronunciation practice, and discussion strategies.

Levels

There are six levels of *Step Up*, CEFR A2+ to C1, Global Scale of English (GSE) 34 to 84.

***Step Up* level**	**GSE**
Step Up A2+	34–43
Step Up B1	41–51
Step Up B1+	49–58
Step Up B2	56–66
Step Up B2+	64–75
Step Up C1	73–84

Two Versions of *Step Up*

Students can study the *Step Up* course in two ways: as a self-study course or as a self-study plus course, which is the self-study course combined with a teacher-led class. As a self-study course, each level of *Step Up* takes students 18 hours to complete, though this may vary as it is self-paced. The teacher-led course provides 14 hours of class time, with additional resources and extension activities available in the Teaching Notes, which would extend class time.

Student's Components

	Self-study course	**Self-study plus course**
Online Course	✓	✓
Coursebook + eBook or eBook only	✗	✓
Resources (online)	✓	✓

Teacher's Components

	Self-study plus course
Coursebook and/or eBook	✓
Access to the Online Course	✓
Teaching Notes	✓
Resources (online)	✓

The Online Course

Students study the following 12 modules, of which the first nine are **personal and social capabilities** and the last three are job-seeking skills:

Module 1 Communication 1	**Module 2** Communication 2	**Module 3** Goal Setting
Module 4 Teamwork	**Module 5** Critical Thinking	**Module 6** Leadership
Module 7 Self-Management	**Module 8** Wellness	**Module 9** Social Responsibility
Module 10 Job Search	**Module 11** Branding	**Module 12** Interviewing

Each module has an employability skills coach—an animated character—who takes the students through the 10 steps of the module. Step 11 is a progress check; it includes a practice test and a graded test. If the student scores at least 70% on every graded test, they are given access to the final exam. If they score at least 80% on this assessment, they receive a certificate of completion.

For a closer look at the online course, please see the Online Module Walkthrough in the Teacher Resources.

Coursebook/eBook

The Coursebook/eBook is made up of two main sections: the modules and the back matter.

The Modules

Welcome Module

The Coursebook begins with a Welcome Module, which is comprised of four sections to:

- help students get to know each other and form a community of learners
- provide students with useful language they need to work effectively in class
- help students navigate the Coursebook so they get the most out of it
- introduce students to the 12 employability skills coaches they meet in the online course.

The 12 Employability Skills Modules

Following the Welcome Module are the 12 employability skills modules, corresponding to each module in the online course. Students need to do each online module before they come to class. In class, you guide them through each module to reinforce what they have learned online, to deepen their understanding of the material, and to share how they can apply what they have learned to their own lives.

Back Matter

There are four sections in the back of the Coursebook and eBook:

- *Check your understanding* enables students to demonstrate they have understood the material they have studied online and gives them an opportunity to clear up any misunderstandings at the beginning of a class.
- *Discussion strategies* provide students with four different sets of strategies that can help them engage in class. These include how to work with others; clarify what you hear or clarify what you say; get and stay involved in the discussion; and organize your ideas. Audio models enable students to practice their pronunciation.
- *Vocabulary practice* gives students additional practice with the vocabulary they have learned in the online course. The first activity is a word puzzle, and the second activity uses the target words from the puzzle in context. The answers are provided in the eBook and in the Resources.
- *The Glossary* provides the definitions of some words or phrases printed in light brown in the Coursebook to facilitate understanding.

Flexibility

While the sequence of the modules is fixed in the coursebook, you can change the sequence to meet the needs of your students. You may want to have the class review the scope and sequence and vote on which modules to do first. If you change the sequence, we suggest you create a syllabus and upload it to the platform.

Resources for Students

All audio and video files for the online course and all audio files for the coursebook are accessible within the activities in the course. In addition, these audio and video files are also available in the Resources, to allow students to watch or listen whenever they wish without going to the lesson itself. Also included in the Resources are the reading texts, as well as answer keys to the *Vocabulary practice* in the Coursebook.

Resources for Teachers

Teaching Notes

There are general teaching notes to help you get the most out of the course. Then there are notes for each module that begin with an overview of the online module that synopsizes what the students have learned online. Following the overview are teaching notes for each step in the coursebook, including tips, extensions, culture notes, and more.

Module Walkthroughs

There is also a module walkthrough that visually describes a module and the underlying pedagogy for both the online course and the coursebook.

Platform Support

To help you navigate the platform and use all the tools available, there is a guided tour when you first log on to Pearson English Connect. In addition, you will find numerous resources under the "Help" button to orient you to the platform. And to get in touch with support, you can click on Help>Documentation>Contact Support.

Welcome

① In the classroom

A Get to know your classmates

Play the Name Game.

B Useful language

Complete the conversations with sentences from the box. Then listen and check your answers.

a ~~Could you explain that?~~	**d** I'm sorry. What page?
b Did you say a pen?	**e** What's the word for this in English?
c Do you mean first we should work alone?	**f** What I mean is you shouldn't read aloud.

C Role play

PAIRS Choose a conversation from 1B and role play it. Use different information.

② Learn about your book

1 How many modules are in the course?

a 5 **b** 9 **c** 11 **d** 12

2 How many steps are in each module?

a 6 **b** 7 **c** 8 **d** 9

3 Look at this icon on page 5. It tells you to go to page 68. Read what is on that page. How can you use that information?

DISCUSSION STRATEGIES
Go to page 68.

____

4 On page 5, Exercise C says Check your understanding. Go to page 54. What is on that page?

a questions to test vocabulary
b questions to ask my teacher
c questions to review the Online Course
d questions to ask my partner

5 Look through Module 1. Which Steps in the book refer to Steps in the Online Course?

a Steps 1, 2, and 3
b Steps 2, 5, and 7
c Steps 3, 4, and 6
d Steps 5, 6, and 7

6 Look at the I-can statement after Step 7 in each module, for example

I can identify successful communication skills. ☐

What is it for?

____

7 What will you find on pages 72–83?

a listening practice
b grammar practice
c vocabulary practice
d pronunciation practice

8 What will you find on pages 86–87?

a a glossary
b listening activities
c vocabulary practice
d an audio script

To find the answers for CHECK YOUR UNDERSTANDING and VOCABULARY PRACTICE you can look in your ebook or use the answer key in the Student's Resources online.

Meet Your Employability Skills Coaches

MODULE 1
Greetings! I'm Dr. Jabu Cele. I have my doctorate in communications and I'm a senior vice president at one of the world's top marketing companies.

MODULE 2
Hi there! I'm Emma Lu, and I'll be your coach for the Communication 2 module. I'm a corporate teamwork coach.

MODULE 3
Hello there. I'm Zehra Teke and I'll be your Employability Skills coach for the module about Goal Setting. I'm a business consultant with a master's degree in management.

MODULE 4
Hello! My name is Kristine Ross. I'm the human resources manager for a large, international company. I'll be your coach for the Teamwork module.

MODULE 5
Hello. My name is Marek Kamiński. I'm an investigative journalist and I'll be your Employability Skills coach for the Critical Thinking module.

MODULE 6
Hi, I'm Sonia Lopez. I'll be your coach for the Leadership module. I'm the Chief Executive Officer—the CEO—of the Alacarte Restaurant Group.

MODULE 7
Hello, my name is Felix Becker. I'm a professional certified life coach and I'll be your coach for the Self-Management module.

MODULE 8
Hello and welcome to the Wellness module. I'll be your Employability Skills coach. My name is Kai Sugimoto. I have a PhD in psychology and I do research on health and wellness.

MODULE 9
Hello, there. My name is Ana Silva. I'm the coordinator of social responsibilty for a large company and I am your coach for the Social Responsibilty module.

MODULE 10
Hi. Welcome to the Branding module. I'm Rakesh Patel, and I'm your Employability Skills coach. I work in marketing.

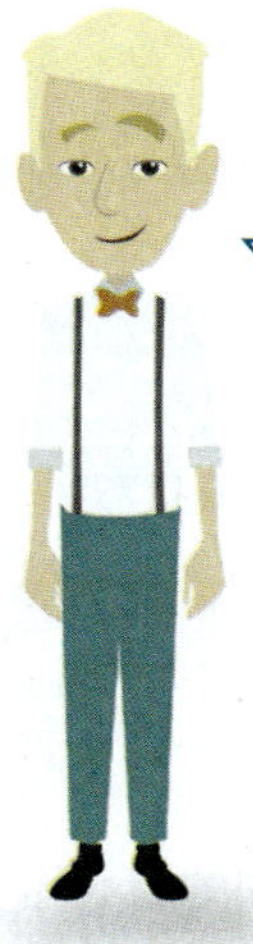

MODULE 11
Hello! Welcome. I'm Justin Roy, and I'm your coach for the Job Search module. I'm a career advice blogger and my goal is to help people find their dream jobs.

MODULE 12
Hi. My name is Aisha Omar. I'm a career counselor at the U.S. Department of Labor and I'll be your coach for the Interviewing module.

MODULE 1

Communication 1

How to Communicate Successfully

DISCUSSION STRATEGIES

Go to page 68.

Step 1 Get started

A Refresh your memory! Watch the *What You'll Learn* video.

B Look at the photos. People at work communicate differently. How do you communicate most often at work or in school? How do you prefer to communicate? Why?

C Check your understanding. Go to page 54.

Step ② Tell your story

A THINK In your online course, you thought about a communication experience you had that went well or did not go well. Listen to the example.

B PAIRS Discuss your story.

C SHARE Tell your story to the class.

Step ③ Activate your knowledge

A PAIRS Read the two scenarios that show different communication breakdowns. Discuss the questions for each scenario.

1 Sam works as a web designer for a home goods company. The laptop he uses for work is getting old and slow, so Sam would like his employer to give him a new one. A new laptop will help him do his work more quickly. It will also allow him to get better software, which will make his designs better. He wants to talk to his boss, Kara, about this.

Sam: Hey, Kara.
Kara: Hi, Sam. What's up?
Sam: Well, I'm working on the new designs. They're a lot bigger now because we've added videos and some new menus.
Kara: Yes?
Sam: Yeah, well, it's taking me a long time. My computer is kind of slow.
Kara: Oh, I see. Well, we have time. You don't need to finish the design for another couple of weeks.
Sam: OK.

1 What is Sam's message? Did he make it clear?
2 Did Sam choose the best medium to deliver his message?
3 How is Sam's delivery?

2 Jia is a customer care specialist at a phone store. She had the following text exchange with her manager, Marie. Marie was not happy.

Jia: well that was bad
Marie: I'm sorry, who is this?
Jia: haha oops it's Jia! I got a new number – forgot to tell you. U remember that lady with the red hair? she just got super mad about the prices going up
Marie: Are you talking about a customer?
Jia: 👍
Marie: Jia, if one of our customers is angry, I want to know about it. Can you please come to my office and explain what happened?
Jia: Well not much really. She came to ask for a new mobile contract because the old one ends soon but now more 💰 so she got 😡
Marie: Can you please come to my office?
Jia: now?
Marie: Yes, now.

1 What is Jia's message? Did she make it clear?
2 Did Jia choose the best medium to deliver her message?
3 How is Jia's delivery?

B PAIRS Together, think about the advice you could give Sam and Jia to make their communication successful. Take notes.

C SHARE Discuss the mistakes you think Sam and Jia made and present to the class your ideas for improving their communication. Take notes while others are presenting. Can you add anything to your list?

Step 4 Take away

A THINK Think about your communication in the last few days at work or in school. Take notes about one spoken or written example in the chart below.

Communication situation	*Meeting at work*	
Was my message clear and simple?	*Yes—I took notes before the meeting*	
Who was my audience?	*Company employees in a different city*	
What was the medium?	*Video conference*	
How was my delivery?	*OK—I had to repeat a couple of things*	
Was this communication successful?	*Yes—I think everyone understood me and there were no problems*	
What should I do differently next time?	*Tell people when they can ask questions*	

B PAIRS Compare your charts. Talk about why the communication examples were successful or not successful.

C SHARE As a class, discuss which kinds of communication problems are the most common.

Step 5 Project

PAIRS In your online course, you took notes about people's communication skills on TV. Using your notes, discuss what you found. Read the example.

I watched an interview of two scientists who study oceans. I'd say the style was polite but not too formal. The scientists shared a lot of information which they explained in a simple way so the audience could understand it. From this I learned that it's important to think about your message and present it clearly.

Step 6 Talk!

PAIRS There are many different kinds of communication problems in the workplace. Read the information and then discuss the questions.

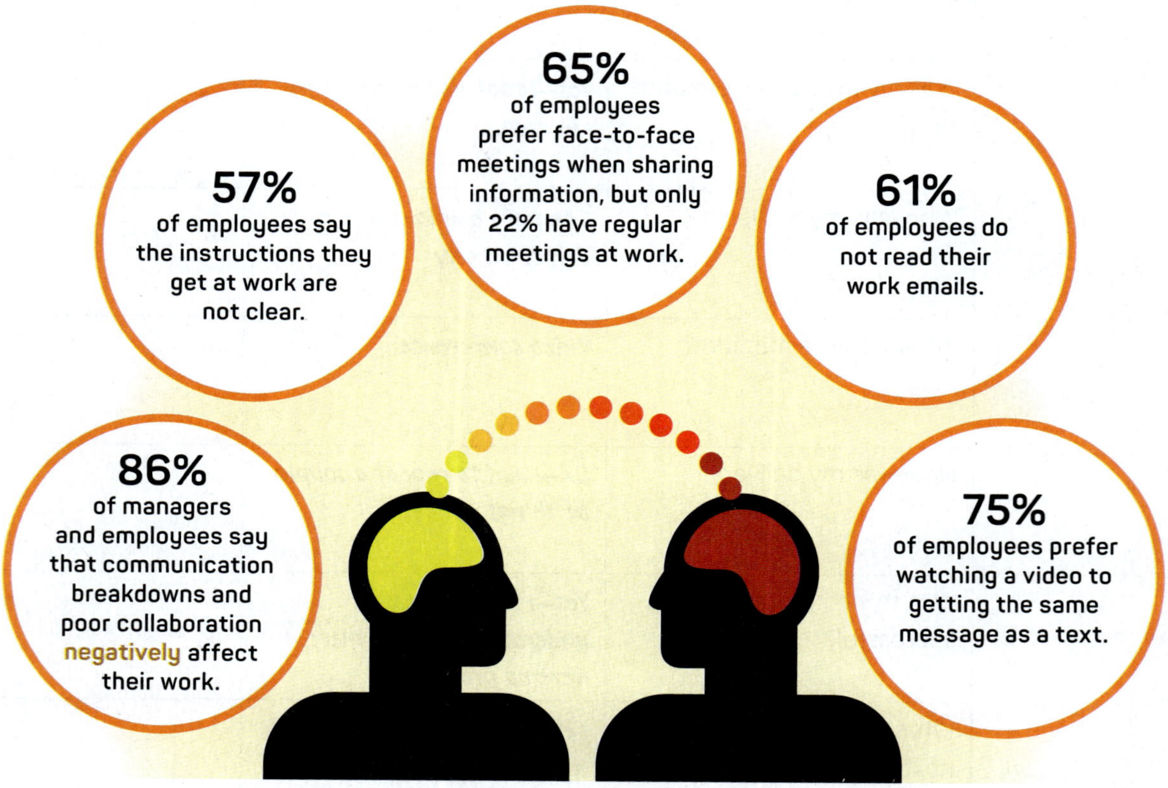

- Do any of these facts surprise you? Why or why not?
- Have you had any of these experiences?
- What other problems can cause communication breakdowns?

Step 7 Going forward

A PAIRS In your online course, you reflected on how you could improve your communication skills. Discuss. Listen to the example.

B SHARE Present your ideas to the class.

VOCABULARY PRACTICE Go to page 72.

I can identify successful communication skills. ☐

MODULE 2

Communication 2

Effective Communication at Work

DISCUSSION STRATEGIES
Go to page 68.

Step 1 Get started

A Refresh your memory! Watch the *What You'll Learn* video.

B Look at the photos. Read the man's body language. What is he communicating in each image?

C Check your understanding. Go to page 55.

Step ② Tell your story

A THINK In your online course, you thought about a time you had to use your communication skills at work or at school. Were you successful? Listen to the example.

B PAIRS Discuss your story.

C SHARE Tell your story to the class.

Step ③ Activate your knowledge

A PAIRS Read the comic. Talk about the communication errors each person makes. Pay attention to whether they are listening to each other, what type of statements they are using, and how they are managing their emotions and body language. Take notes.

B PAIRS Read the scenarios. Work together to write a conversation for each one. Practice the conversations.

1

A boss is giving instructions to an employee. The boss wants the employee to call a client to arrange a meeting for next week. The employee needs to set up the meeting, reserve the meeting room, and report back to the boss with the date and time. The employee asks questions to confirm understanding.

Boss:	(Gives instructions)
Employee:	(Repeats back, but is not completely correct)
Boss:	(Corrects employee)
Employee:	(Repeats back correctly)
Boss:	Exactly!

2

A customer is complaining to a salesclerk. The customer bought an expensive item that broke or stopped working very quickly. It is too late to return the item, but the customer wants his money back.

Customer: (Angrily complains)
Clerk: (Expresses understanding, asks for more information)
Customer: (Continues complaint)
Clerk: (Listens carefully, offers to get the manager)
Customer: (Thanks clerk, calms down)

C SHARE **Role-play your conversations for the class. Take notes while others are presenting and give each other feedback.**

Step 4 Take away

A PAIRS **Create a checklist with tips for effective communication at work. Think of three examples for each communication skill.**

Listen carefully	**Manage your emotions**
• *When you don't understand directions, ask the speaker to say them again, more slowly.* • ________ • ________	• ________ • ________ • ________
Use *I* statements	**Control your body language**
• ________ • ________ • ________	• ________ • ________ • ________

B SHARE **Compare your checklist with another pair's. What can you add to your checklist?**

Step 5 Project

PAIRS **In your online course, you interviewed people about their communication skills in the workplace. Discuss their responses. Read the example.**

I interviewed three friends. They all said that paying attention to your body language is very important. One person said that your body language is a good way to show people that you're interested in them, especially in video meetings. She explained that sometimes people forget that everyone can see them and they look bored. Her advice was to always look at the screen and make eye contact to show that you're paying attention.

Step 6 Talk!

PAIRS A recent survey asked employees about annoying co-worker habits. Read some of the survey results. What do you think is the worst habit in each category? Talk about your own experiences. What did you do about it?

Worst co-worker telephone habits
- talks too loudly
- takes personal calls
- doesn't use headphones during calls in an open office

Worst co-worker personal habits
- eats loudly at his or her desk
- coughs or sneezes without covering mouth
- wears too much perfume

Worst co-worker meeting habits
- texts/chats during meetings
- talks loudly when others are trying to talk
- holds meetings that are not necessary

Worst co-worker email habits
- sends emails that are not necessary
- uses "reply all" to answer whole-company emails
- uses company email to try to sell things to co-workers

Step 7 Going forward

A PAIRS In your online course, you reflected on how you could improve your workplace communication skills. Discuss. Listen to the example.

B SHARE Present your ideas to the class.

VOCABULARY PRACTICE Go to page 73.

I can identify effective oral communication skills in the workplace. ☐

3

MODULE

Goal Setting

SMART Goals

DISCUSSION STRATEGIES

Go to page 68.

Step 1

Get started

A Refresh your memory! Watch the *What You'll Learn* video.

B Look at the photo. What do you think this person's goal was? Do you or anyone you know have a goal like this one?

C Check your understanding. Go to page 56.

Step ② Tell your story

A THINK In your online course, you thought about a goal you had in the past. Did you achieve it? Why or why not? Listen to the example.

B PAIRS Discuss your story.

C SHARE Tell your story to the class.

Step ③ Take away

PAIRS Paul is a sales representative. This is one of his SMART goals:

Find three new customers each week by making ten calls by 5 P.M. every day.

Complete the chart. Write the definitions of each feature and use Paul's goal to write examples.

	Definition	Example
Specific	*includes details that are explained in a clear way*	*find new customers each week by making calls*
Measurable		
Achievable		
Relevant		
Time-bound		

Step ④ Activate your knowledge

A PAIRS Read the scenarios showing different people's goals. Check the boxes that apply to the goal. Then discuss why the goal is not SMART. Work together to rewrite the goals as SMART goals.

1

Tuyet works as an administrative assistant. She was out of the office for a few days and has a huge amount of work to do: 25 emails and 8 phone calls to respond to, office supplies to order, and 10 appointments to schedule. This amount of work would usually take her about 2 days. Of course, she also has new work coming in every day that she needs to finish. Today is Monday.

HER GOAL *Finish all work by Tuesday afternoon.*

☐ Specific ☐ Measurable ☐ Achievable ☐ Relevant ☐ Time-bound

SMART goal: ______________________________

____

2 Murat is a marketing specialist. He has had the same job at a technology company for four years, and he really likes it. But now the company is closing the office he works in, and he is going to lose his job in two months. He should start looking for new work.

HIS GOAL *Complete job applications.*

☐ Specific ☐ Measurable ☐ Achievable ☐ Relevant ☐ Time-bound

SMART goal: ______________________________

____

3 

Alma wants to have a career in medicine. She is good at science subjects, but is having difficulty with her chemistry class. She took two tests so far and her highest score was 60%. This semester she isn't spending enough time on chemistry. She missed two classes, doesn't take careful notes, and often does not study until the night before the test. To continue her medical studies, she needs to pass this class. There are two more tests until the end of the semester.

HER GOAL *Study hard and do better on the next test.*

☐ Specific ☐ Measurable ☐ Achievable ☐ Relevant ☐ Time-bound

SMART goal: ______________________________

____

4 Karla is an HR manager. Her company is sending her to Germany for a year to help open a new office there. She is going to help the local HR department hire and train new employees. Her company offered to pay for her language course. She is very excited about the opportunity, but is leaving in five months and only speaks basic German.

HER GOAL *Improve German skills by the time I leave.*

☐ Specific ☐ Measurable ☐ Achievable ☐ Relevant ☐ Time-bound

SMART goal: ______________________________

____

B **GROUPS OF 4** **Share the new goals you wrote with another pair. Analyze the goals to make sure they are SMART. Decide which pair has the best goal for each person. Then write those goals in the chart.**

1 Tuyet	
2 Murat	
3 Alma	
4 Karla	

Step 5 Project

PAIRS In your online course, you wrote two goals you would like to achieve. Share your goals and explain why they are SMART. Listen to your partner's goals. If you see any way to improve them, offer suggestions. Read the example.

My job is ending in a couple of months, so I need to prepare for a job search. I want to share my website with employers, but the design and most of the information on it is old. My goal is to spend two hours a week over the next month working on the site. My goal is achievable because I have some free time on the weekends, and it's time-bound, measurable, and relevant. But I'm not sure if it's specific enough. Maybe I should set more specific goals like, "replace the old photos and update the menus."

Step 6 Talk!

PAIRS Many people set goals for themselves at the beginning of the new year, that is, they make New Year's resolutions. Look at the most popular goals of a recent survey about New Year's resolutions. Discuss the questions.

- Do any of these resolutions surprise you? Can you add any others to this list?
- Why do people make resolutions?
- Why do you think it is so difficult for people to keep their resolutions?

Step 7 Going forward

A PAIRS In your online course, you reflected on how you could improve your goal setting. Discuss. Listen to the example.

B SHARE Present your ideas to the class.

VOCABULARY PRACTICE
Go to page 74.

I can explain the importance of setting SMART goals and describe how to create them. ☐

4 MODULE

Teamwork

Being a Team Player

DISCUSSION STRATEGIES
Go to page 68.

Step 1 Get started

A Refresh your memory! Watch the *What You'll Learn* video.

B Look at the photo. What is this team's goal? How could they work together successfully?

C Check your understanding. Go to page 57.

Step 2 Tell your story

A THINK In your online course, you thought about a time you worked on a group project at work, at school, or in your personal life. Was the experience good or bad? Listen to the example.

B PAIRS Discuss your story.

C SHARE Tell your story to the class.

Step 3 Take away

A PAIRS Review your notes from the online module. Complete each list with a tip from the box.

How can you improve your teamwork skills?

Be responsible	Be kind and respectful	Have the same goal	Be flexible
Know your strengths and weaknesses		Communicate about how things are going	

1 ____________
- Stay focused.
- Keep your eye on the goal.

2 ____________
- Know your role.
- Do your part well and on time.

3 ____________
- Encourage others to share ideas.
- Come to an agreement.

4 ____________
- Listen to others.
- Be open to different ways of working.

5 ____________
- Use your skills to help the group.
- Encourage your teammates to use their skills, too.

6 ____________
- Let others know if you are having problems.
- Ask for help if you need it.

B SHARE Check your answers with the class.

Step 4 Activate your knowledge

A PAIRS Read about working in teams and then answer the questions.

1

Another Successful Cleanup!

Thanks so much to everyone who gave their time to our 5th Community Cleanup! The teams did an amazing job and picked up 1,687 pounds of trash. The team from the local youth center picked up the most, including an old bicycle and 15 car tires. The children at ABC Nursery also did a great job! They picked up 8 pounds of trash all around the park.

A special thank-you also to the gardening volunteers. The Green Corner shop donated 45 plants to make our streets more beautiful. And when the volunteers were planting the flowers, they saw that the front of the library on Broad Street didn't look very good. So, they found some brushes and paint and took care of that problem, too. Now the street looks great!

Thank you to everyone and congratulations on your beautiful neighborhood!

1 What was the community's goal?
2 Why was their teamwork successful?

2

Sarah Meecham offers advice for all of your workplace problems.

Team Fail

Dear Sarah: My manager at work created a team of seven people to research information about changes that she wants to make in the company. She asked each of us to find information on a different topic and then to meet together to discuss what we learned and decide how we would present the information to her.

Our first meeting was TERRIBLE. One of the team members kept saying that he should make the presentation to the manager after we finish the research. The problem was that he hadn't done any work at all! He wanted to make the presentation to make it look like he was leading the team. This made everyone else really angry because we wanted to make the presentation as a group. After all, it was a team project. By the time the meeting ended, we still hadn't agreed on who would make the final presentation, and we hadn't even discussed any of the things we found when doing our research! What should I do?

Sad Team Leader

1 What is the team's goal?
2 What are the problems with this team?
3 If you were Sarah, what advice would you give the team leader?

3

Trent

Well, last night was not good! I usually work very well with my co-workers at the theater. We all want to make sure everyone who comes to an event has a great time. I'm responsible for the food and drinks we sell during the shows, and my co-workers always help out if we're busy or if I need something at the last minute. But last night there was a special party before the show, but no one told me. I didn't have enough food, so I had to go shopping and then wasn't ready in time when the guests arrived. I felt so bad!

Likes 27 Comments 8

1 Why does this team usually work well?
2 What went wrong last night?
3 What should the team do to prevent future problems like this one?

B SHARE Discuss your answers with another pair.

Step 5 Project

PAIRS In your online course, you did a survey of your friends, family, and co-workers about their experience working in teams. Compare your survey with a partner's. Work together to summarize your results. Read the example.

Everyone I spoke to liked working in a team, and everyone had similar experiences with teams. Some teams worked well and some teams didn't. They all said that having just one difficult person on a team can cause a lot of problems. My mother talked about a group she worked with where one person was always talking and not listening to anyone else. The whole team felt they weren't making any progress, so they made that co-worker leave the group. It helped, but the team felt bad about the situation. My mother said that maybe a better idea would be to talk to that person about the problem first.

Step 6 Talk!

PAIRS Read about how animals live and work in teams. Then discuss the questions.

Busy Bees

Bees are famous for how much work they get done. A hive—a place where bees live—can have as many as 60,000 bees, and each one has a job to do. Some of them clean the hive, some feed young bees, and some look for food. Together, they work to make the hive a success.

Howling Wolves

Wolves live in close groups called packs that work together to hunt and raise their young. They use their loud howling (crying) over long distances to tell each other when danger is near, or when there is an animal to hunt. Their howls also help them find members of their pack.

Flying Geese

When geese fly long distances, they form a V in the sky, with a leader in the front. But the leader isn't always the same bird. When one leader gets tired, another bird will move into its place. By changing leaders this way, geese are able to fly as many as 3,000 miles (4,800 kilometers) in a day.

- How do animals benefit from working in teams?
- Do you know other examples of animal teamwork?
- What could people learn from these animal teams?

Step 7 Going forward

A PAIRS In your online course, you reflected on how you could improve your teamwork skills. Discuss. Listen to the example.

B SHARE Present your ideas to the class.

VOCABULARY PRACTICE
Go to page 75.

I can explain the importance of teamwork and describe the skills of an effective team. ☐

5

MODULE

Critical Thinking

Critical Thinking Skills

DISCUSSION STRATEGIES

Go to page 68.

Step ① Get started

A Refresh your memory! Watch the *What You'll Learn* video.

B Look at the photo. What do you do when you have to make an important decision or solve a problem?

C Check your understanding. Go to page 58.

Step ② Tell your story

A THINK In your online course, you thought about times in your life when you had to think critically. Listen to the example.

B PAIRS Discuss your story.

C SHARE Tell your story to the class.

Step ③ Take away

A THINK Review your notes from the online module. What do you know about the critical thinking process? Complete the information about each step.

What is critical thinking?	Critical thinking is a set of skills you use to analyze, evaluate, and make [1] __________ based on information from different [2] __________.
Step 1	[3] __________ information from different sources and try to understand it from different [4] __________.
Step 2	Analyze and evaluate the information with an [5] __________ mind. Separate [6] __________ from opinions. Check that sources have [7] __________ to back up their claims.
Step 3	Combine Steps 1 and 2 and make a [8] __________.
Step 4	[9] __________ and change your thinking process, if necessary.

B PAIRS Compare your charts. Make changes as necessary.

Step ④ Activate your knowledge

A PAIRS Read the scenarios. Use your critical thinking skills to answer the questions.

1 You own a chain of supermarkets and are thinking about changing the hours from 8 A.M. to 8 P.M. daily to 8 A.M. to 12 A.M. You need to find out if this is a good business decision.

How will you learn about different viewpoints?	
What factual information should you gather?	
How will you make your decision?	
How will you review your decision?	

2 You are members of the town council. There have been a lot of accidents at this street corner. It is dangerous for both cars and people who need to cross the street. You need to put either a stop sign or a traffic light there. The council needs to make a decision.

How will you learn about different viewpoints?	
What factual information should you gather?	
How will you make your decision?	
How will you review your decision?	

3 Your manager wants to buy a new computer system for the office. It is your team's job to research the possibilities and decide what to buy.

What sources should you consider?	
How will you learn about different viewpoints?	
What factual information should you gather?	
What sources of factual information should you trust?	
What kinds of information might cause you to change your mind?	

B SHARE **Share your ideas with another pair's. Choose the best answers.**

Step 5 Project

PAIRS In your online course, you evaluated an issue in your community and thought about a plan for how to fix it. Explain the issue and describe your thinking process. Read the example.

One problem in my community is that a lot of the streets near the school don't have sidewalks. This means that children are walking in the street. Also, there aren't any bike lanes for bicycles. I looked at this problem from both the town council's and the people's viewpoints. I found out that the town council doesn't have money for new sidewalks. But then I looked at how other towns handle this issue. I found out that it's much less expensive to paint bike lanes on the streets, and then add another line on the inside for people who are walking. It's not a perfect solution, but the council could afford it, and it would be safer for the children.

Step 6 Talk!

PAIRS How important do you think critical skills are in the workplace? Look at the survey results below. Discuss the questions.

- Do employers think that their employees have good critical thinking skills?
- Why do employers and recent graduates disagree about the graduates' critical thinking skills?
- Why do employers say critical thinking is so important? Do you think it is true for all jobs?

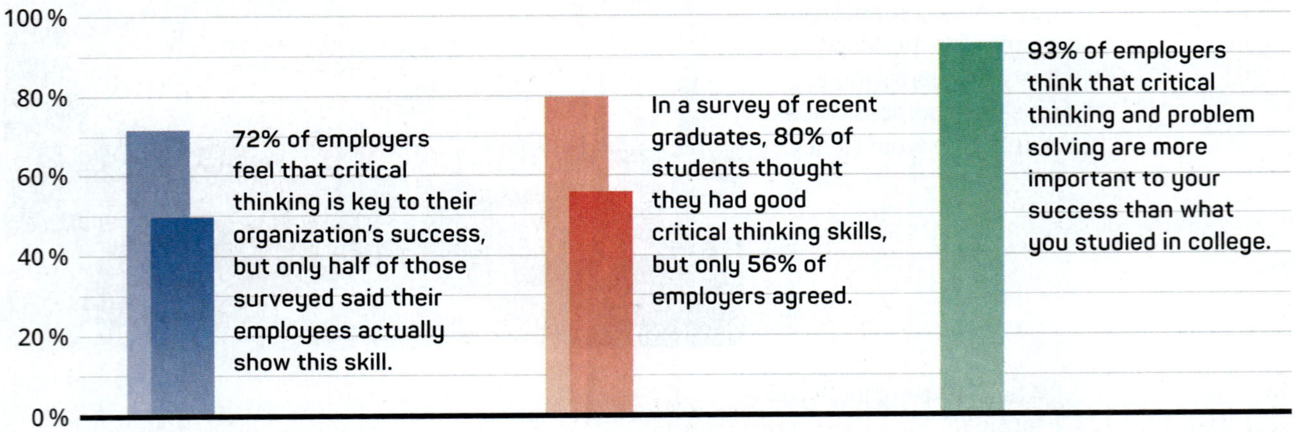

Step 7 Going forward

A PAIRS In your online course, you reflected on how you could improve your critical thinking skills. Discuss. Listen to the example.

B SHARE Present your ideas to the class.

VOCABULARY PRACTICE
Go to page 76.

I can explain and describe the steps in the critical thinking process. ☐

6 MODULE

Leadership

Leadership Skills

DISCUSSION STRATEGIES

Go to page 68.

Step 1 Get started

A Refresh your memory. Watch the *What You'll Learn* video.

B Look at the photo. Have you ever worked in small groups at school or work? Did your group have a good leader? What does a good leader do in a group?

C Check your understanding. Go to page 59.

Step ② Tell your story

A THINK In your online course, you thought about a person you knew who was a good or a bad leader. What was your experience with this person? Listen to the example.

B PAIRS Discuss your story.

C SHARE Tell your story to the class.

Step ③ Activate your knowledge

A THINK Read the stories. Take notes about how the employees can use their leadership skills to solve the problems.

1

Ben is a server at a restaurant. Every night, he and two other servers need to make sure the restaurant is ready for the next day. One of the servers is not helping, and the manager is angry that the work is not finished on time.

2

Kara is the manager at a clothing store. She recently decided to have one employee stand near the door to say "hello" to customers as they come in. She thinks this will help customers feel more welcome. Today, two employees told her that they think this is a bad idea. They said the person at the door does not help customers and that now there are not enough people working in other areas of the store.

3

Tom is a receptionist in an office. There is a large cabinet where pens, paper, and other items are stored. Everyone in the office uses this cabinet, but it is not anyone's job to check if any items are running out. All the employees, including Tom, are busy, and the cabinet is almost empty.

4 Gayle works in the IT department at a large company. The company is changing its software, and the IT department is very busy. Employees are calling all day asking for help and complaining about the changes, and everyone in IT is working long hours. They are all tired and feeling bad, and some are talking about quitting.

____

____

B PAIRS Discuss how each person can show his or her leadership skills.

C SHARE Tell the class your ideas.

Step 4 Take away

PAIRS Read the quotes from job interviewees and match them with the correct skill or skills.

1 I can accept feedback. ______
2 I am trustworthy and honest. ______
3 I can motivate others. ______
4 I respect others. ______
5 I work well with others. ______
6 I have good ideas. ______
7 I am willing to make decisions. ______
8 I am willing to take responsibility. ______

a *My marketing team was working on a product video for several weeks. People kept trying to make little changes, but it wasn't getting any better. No one wanted to stop working on it because of all the time we'd already spent. I was the one who said, "It's over. Let's throw everything away and start again." It was the right choice, and our new plan worked much better.*

b *When I worked at the supermarket, I had the keys to the building. It was my job to turn on the alarm and lock the doors every night.*

c *As a member of the social media team, I met with managers, employees, current customers, and potential customers. Meeting all these people and listening to their ideas was a big part of my job—and I loved it.*

d *At the hotel, we had visitors from all over the world. I enjoyed meeting people from different places who spoke different languages. I found that if you're interested in people and you're nice to them, you can communicate quite well.*

e *One year, my sales team wasn't doing very well. So, I started meeting with team members often in order to help them set goals. And when they met those goals, I told them they were doing a good job. Our sales went up quite a bit after that.*

f *Our company sold toys. One time, a message was sent to many of our customers with the wrong sale dates. I contacted them right away with the correct information. My boss was happy that I took care of the problem without waiting for anyone to ask me.*

g *At my last job, the manager evaluated us every year. I was always happy to learn about how I could improve. I used the information to do a better job.*

h *When I first started working at the furniture company, their website and their ordering system were a mess. I developed a better design for the site and a new way to do the ordering. This helped us to get more customers and to serve our customers faster.*

Step 5 Project

A PAIRS **In your online course, you researched a famous leader and explained what made him or her a good leader. Tell your partner why you thought the person was a good leader. Read the example.**

I wrote about Greta Thunberg, the leader of a youth movement against climate change. She's a good leader because she does what she wants others to do. When she was 15 years old, she started a climate protest all by herself. Instead of going to school, she protested in front of the Swedish Parliament. Soon students all over the world joined her. But Greta didn't just ask governments to act, she also asked her own parents to change how they do things. The next year, she traveled to North America to meet with environmentalists and attend climate protests. Flying is one cause of climate change, so she traveled by boat. To me, she has great leadership qualities.

B SHARE **Tell the class about the leader you researched.**

Step 6 Talk!

GROUPS OF 3–4 **Look at these leaders who have changed their country and the world. What do you know about them?**

Indira Gandhi
1917–1984

Nelson Mandela
1918–2013

Alexander the Great
356 BCE–323 BCE

Cleopatra
69 BCE–30 BCE

- If you became a leader as important as one of those above, what would you do to make your country or the world a better place?
- How would you do it and why?

Step 7 Going forward

A PAIRS **In your online course, you reflected on ways to improve your leadership skills. Discuss. Listen to the example.**

B SHARE **Present your ideas to the class.**

VOCABULARY PRACTICE
Go to page 77.

I can describe the skills needed to lead people effectively. ☐

7

MODULE

Self-Management

Time Management

DISCUSSION STRATEGIES

Go to page 68.

Step 1 Get started

A Refresh your memory! Watch the *What You'll Learn* video.

B Look at the photo. Sometimes, we have to do several things at the same time. We call this *juggling time*. Do you ever have to juggle your time? Explain.

C Check your understanding. Go to page 60.

Step 2 Tell your story

A THINK In your online course, you thought about your self-management skills. When were you successful or not successful at self-management? Listen to the example.

B PAIRS Discuss your story.

C SHARE Tell your story to the class.

Step 3 Take away

THINK Complete the chart with a definition for each time-management tool and an example of how to use it. Think of an event at home, school, or work that you need to plan for. How could you use each tool to plan it?

Time-management tool	What is it?	Example
To-do list	*a list of your goals for a week, month, or day*	
Backward planning		
ABC grid		

Step 4 Activate your knowledge

A THINK Read and listen to the scenarios then complete the time-management tools.

1

Fran's project

- ______________________
- ______________________
- ______________________
- ______________________
- ______________________
- ______________________

Fran is a caterer. She and her sister make food for parties and meetings. Their business is going very well, and Fran wants to hire more people to help. She knows that she needs to complete some paperwork for the government, put an advertisement online and interview people, and get some new software for paying the staff. But she is still researching. There may be more steps in the process that she does not know about yet.

2

Ari's project

APRIL						
S	M	T	W	Th	F	S
1	2	3	4	5	6	7
8	9	10	11	12	13	14
15	16	17	18	19	20	21
22	23	24	25	26	27	28
29	30					

Ari is a web designer. It is April 1st, and he has an important deadline for a new website on the 23rd of the month. He needs to plan for someone to take the photos this week and he must get the text from the writer soon after that. Then he needs to finish the design a few days before the deadline so that he has time to check it.

3

Jeff's project

A	B	C

Jeff is a building manager. He needs to prepare an office in a new building. The workers will move in on the 23rd. Jeff knows everything will not be ready by then, but he has to make a plan. There are some very important things to do—he needs to get the big furniture in, get the heating system working, and make sure the lighting and plumbing are working. He will also have to bring in less important things, like the art for the walls and the microwave for the kitchen. And once they move in, he will help the office workers put the furniture where they want it and make any small repairs they need.

B SHARE Share your planning tools with the class.

Step 5 Project

A PAIRS In your online course, you used an ABC grid or a backward-planning calendar to plan an event. Compare your work with a partner. Explain your choices and give each other feedback. Read the example.

I chose a backward-planning calendar for a birthday party. I think it's the most useful way to make sure that everything is done by a certain day. The birthday party is at a restaurant, so the first thing on my calendar is making the restaurant reservation. After that, I will send out invitations because I think people like to make plans in advance. Also, I need to know how many people are coming in case I need to change the reservation.

B SHARE Discuss your choices with the class.

Step 6 Talk!

PAIRS People use many different kinds of planning tools. Some work, some do not. Read the survey results about to-do lists. Then discuss the questions.

41% of to-do list items are never completed.

50% of completed to-do list items are done within a day.

50% of list-writers say that they sometimes write down items they have already completed and then cross them off.

29% of people use code to write part of their to-do list.

- Why are so many items never completed?
- Why are so many items completed so quickly?
- Why do people write items that they have already completed? Have you ever done that?
- Why do some people use code for parts of their list? What do you think they put on those lists?

Step 7 Going forward

A PAIRS In your online course, you reflected on how you could improve your time management skills. Discuss. Listen to the example.

B SHARE Present your ideas to the class.

VOCABULARY PRACTICE
Go to page 78.

I can describe specific strategies for managing and planning my time. ☐

8

MODULE

Wellness

Healthy Habits

DISCUSSION STRATEGIES

Go to page 68.

Step ①

Get started

A Refresh your memory! Watch the *What You'll Learn* video.

B Look at the photo. Do you and people you know exercise? Is it better to work out or to play a sport? Why?

C Check your understanding. Go to page 61.

Step 2 Tell your story

A THINK In your online course, you thought about a time when your habits had a good or bad effect on your health. Listen to the example.

B PAIRS Discuss your story.

C SHARE Tell your story to the class.

Step 3 Activate your knowledge

A THINK Dr. Eva Medina answers questions about health. Read the letters. Take notes in the chart about each writer's habits.

YOUR HEALTH

Are You Healthy? Ask the Doctor!

Dr. Eva Medina

1 Dear Dr. Medina,

I'm hoping you can give me some advice. I'm a 20-year-old student. I exercise, I don't drink alcohol, and I try to eat well. But it just seems like I don't have any energy. Sometimes I fall asleep during my 8 A.M. class. That class is only on Tuesdays and Thursdays. I try to go to bed early on Monday and Wednesday nights, but I can't fall asleep. So, I just lie in bed playing games on my phone until I finally get sleepy. On other days my classes are later, so

I usually study until 2 or 3 A.M. And on the weekends, I sleep a lot. But I'm still tired!

Thanks for your help,
Tired Tuan

2 Hi, Doctor.

Please help me with an argument I'm having with my best friend. She says that I'm not healthy because I start every day with just a cup of coffee. But I think she's wrong. I get lots of exercise—I run five miles three times a week! I drink plenty of water throughout the day. And I usually eat a large meal with lots of protein and vegetables right before I go to bed, so I'm not hungry in the morning. Then I'm busy at work until the early afternoon, so I don't have much time to eat.

I do feel pretty tired in the afternoons, but I think that's just because I work hard! So, who's right, me or my friend?

Best,
Running Rita

3 Dear Dr. Medina,

When I was young, I didn't worry about my health, but now that I'm getting older, I want to make sure I have good habits. Here's a typical day of food and exercise for me:

Morning:
1 coffee + 2 slices of toast with butter
30 minutes of aerobic exercise or strength training

Afternoon:
bowl of white rice with vegetables
1 piece of fruit

Evening:
pasta or potatoes with salad

What do you think? Is this a healthy diet? By the way, I don't smoke, but I live in a house with two smokers.

Best,
Careful Carmen

	Good health habits	Bad health habits	Suggestions
Tuan			
Rita			
Carmen			

B PAIRS Compare your answers. Then make suggestions that will improve each person's health. Take notes in the chart.

Step 4 Take away

PAIRS Review your notes from the online module and Step 3. Discuss the importance of good health habits. Complete the diagrams with ideas for how to stay healthy.

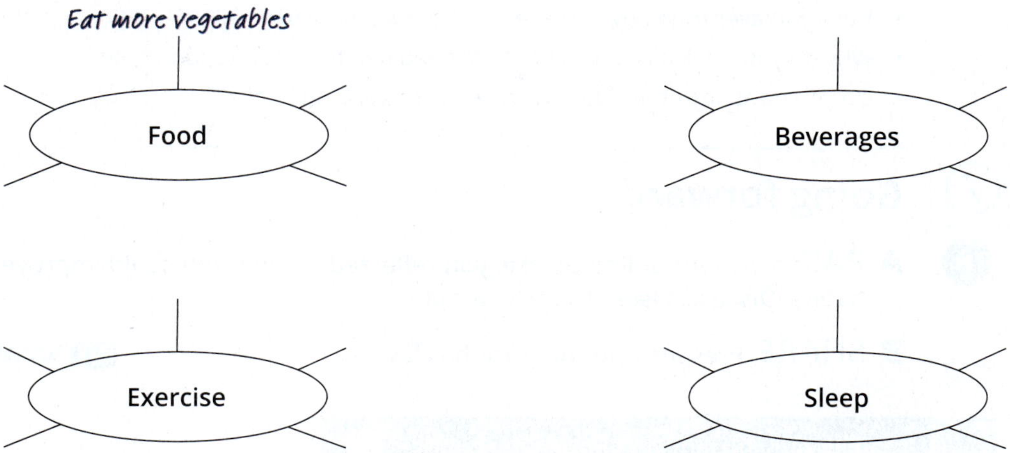

Step 5 Project

A PAIRS In your online course, you took notes about a health app or website. Tell your partner about it. Read the example.

The app I found was a fitness watch. It tells you how many steps you take and keeps track of your heart rate and of how well you sleep at night. You can also put in the food you eat and how much water you drink throughout the day. I think it helps you make healthy food and good exercise choices.

B SHARE Discuss the results of your online search with the class. Decide on which three apps or websites are the favorites.

Step 6 Talk!

PAIRS Habits are hard to change. Read the tips about how to create good habits. Then discuss the questions.

Start small! Pick an easy change, for example five minutes of exercise or one piece of fruit with lunch. Once you have this new habit, then you can add to it.

Use a calendar or reminder app. This will help you remember when it is time to exercise, start preparing a healthy dinner, or go to bed.

Picture the change. Create a picture in your mind. For example, if you are trying to start running, close your eyes and think of what you will wear and where you will go.

Be nice to yourself! Sometimes our habits make us feel bad. But that is not helpful. Instead, think about the things you are doing well and how you will do better in the future.

Remove triggers. Triggers are things that go along with your bad habits. For example, if you usually smoke when you take a coffee break, try drinking tea or water on your break instead.

- Have you ever tried any of these ideas? How did they work?
- Why do you think it is difficult to break bad habits and start good ones?
- Do you have any other ideas on how to create good habits?

Step 7 Going forward

A PAIRS In your online course, you reflected on how you could improve your health habits. Discuss. Listen to the example.

B SHARE Present your ideas to the class.

VOCABULARY PRACTICE
Go to page 79.

I can identify healthy and unhealthy habits. ☐

9 MODULE

Social Responsibility

Personal Responsibility

DISCUSSION STRATEGIES
Go to page 68.

Step 1 Get started

A Refresh your memory! Watch the *What You'll Learn* video.

B Look at the photos. What would be different about working in each type of office? How might your behavior change for each one?

C Check your understanding. Go to page 62.

Step 2 Tell your story

A THINK In your online course, you thought about someone you knew who had bad workplace etiquette. Listen to the example.

B PAIRS Discuss your story.

C SHARE Tell your story to the class.

Step 3 Activate your knowledge

A THINK Read the scenarios and look at the pictures. Which workplace etiquette tips would you give to each person. Take notes.

1 Luz, Kevin, Arif, and Hue are having an online meeting.

Kevin is working from home. He is wearing a T-shirt, and it looks like he didn't comb his hair this morning. His dog keeps coming into the room, and Kevin plays with him while the others are talking.

During the meeting, Luz is texting with another co-worker about a different project. She keeps missing parts of the conversation and saying, "I'm sorry, could you say that again?"

Arif does not like their new manager. He mentions several times that he is very unhappy with the way the new manager is doing things, and he tells his co-workers that he is thinking about quitting the job.

Hue does not like to turn on her camera for meetings. She can see the others, but they can only see a picture and hear her voice.

After 45 minutes, they have not gotten much work done, and they decide to meet again in a few days.

Luz ____________________

Kevin ____________________

Arif ____________________

Hue ____________________

2

Amy and Rolando are new employees at a tech company. Rolando is very friendly and everyone seems to like him. He feels a connection to Amy because they are both new, so he keeps texting her jokes and funny things during the day. This makes Amy very uncomfortable.

Amy is not making friends with her other co-workers, either. Her co-workers often talk about their interests and their lives outside of work, and they bring in personal items for their desks. Amy feels that work is a place for working. She does not like to put anything on her desk, and she never talks about her life outside of work.

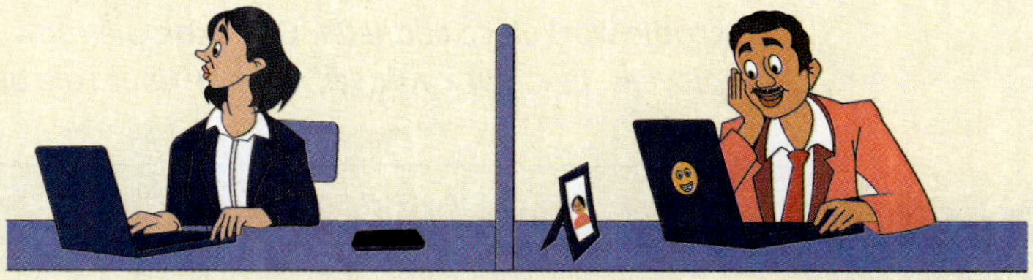

Amy ______________________________

Rolando ______________________________

B PAIRS Work together to write a new scenario about two or three people who are not following workplace etiquette tips.

____

____

____

____

C SHARE Read your scenario to the class.

Step 4 Take away

A THINK Review your notes from the online module and put each habit in the correct column.

Workplace etiquette	
Dos	**Don'ts**
Pay attention to how people communicate	

B PAIRS Check your answers with a partner. Discuss which habits are the most common.

Step 5 Project

PAIRS In your online course, you interviewed people or did research about more tips and examples of good and bad workplace etiquette. Compare your list with a partner. Then combine your lists. Discuss which problems are the worst or most common. Read the example.

I looked up examples online. One bad habit a lot of people have is saying negative things about their co-workers or talking about their co-workers' personal lives. That makes people feel uncomfortable and is terrible workplace etiquette. One example I saw of good workplace etiquette is to be friendly to new employees. Introduce yourself, explain your role at the company and help them to feel comfortable.

Step 6 Talk!

PAIRS Workplace culture changes from company to company. It is also not the same throughout the world. Look at the examples of workstyles and habits from different countries. Then discuss the questions.

In France, if you work for a company with fifty or more employees, there is a law that says you cannot email an employee after the regular working hours or on the weekends. This law was made because studies have shown that in the current digital age it is hard for workers to get away from the workplace. The law was passed to give workers more personal time and less stress.

Many workers in Japan do ten to fifteen minutes of exercise together each morning. The music and exercises called *Radio Taiso*, are on the radio all over the country. It is designed for anyone at any age and it needs no equipment. Companies believe that the exercise will help workers have less stress and feel more connected to each other.

The Swedes believe that coffee breaks, which they call *fika*, are very important. They think that workers feel better and work harder when they take regular breaks. In some Swedish businesses, co-workers get together twice a day, at 9 and 3, to talk, have a drink, and eat something sweet.

At many Egyptian offices, there are waiters who bring coffee, tea, water, and snacks to employees. The company often pays for these items. You can also ask them to do other things for you, like pick up your lunch or medicine from a pharmacy.

- How do you think these workstyles might affect the workplace culture?
- Are these workstyle habits similar or different where you live?
- Talk about which ones you like or do not like.

Step 7 Going forward

A PAIRS In your online course, you reflected on how you could improve your workplace etiquette. Discuss. Listen to the example.

B SHARE Present your ideas to the class.

VOCABULARY PRACTICE Go to page 80.

I can explain the importance of personal social responsibility and describe workplace etiquette. ☐

10 MODULE

Branding

Branding Basics

DISCUSSION STRATEGIES

Go to page 68.

Step 1 Get started

A Refresh your memory! Watch the *What You'll Learn* video.

B Look at the photo. What makes you different from other people; how do you stand out from the crowd?

C Check your understanding. Go to page 63.

Step 2 Tell your story

A THINK In your online course, you thought about someone whose brand you admire. Listen to the example.

B PAIRS Discuss your story.

C SHARE Tell your story to the class.

Step 3 Take away

A PAIRS How should you build your brand? Complete the checklist with the words in the box.

goals	skills	words	strengths	résumé	match
mission	online	different	share	develop	audience

- ☐ Make a list of your __________ and weaknesses.
- ☐ Think about what makes you __________ from other people.
- ☐ Ask people to describe you in a few __________.
- ☐ Think about your experience and your __________.
- ☐ Write down your long-term __________.
- ☐ __________ your brand to your goals.
- ☐ Think about your __________. Who do you want to reach?
- ☐ Write a __________ statement.
- ☐ Make sure that your __________ and cover letter highlight your brand.
- ☐ Look carefully at your __________ presence.
- ☐ Try to meet new people in your field and __________ your personal brand with them.
- ☐ Continue to __________ and revise your brand.

B SHARE Check your answers with another pair's.

Step 4 Activate your knowledge

A PAIRS Meet Lucia. Read and listen to her story. Look at her online presence and read her mission statement. Then answer the questions, and discuss what advice you would give her.

Lucia's story:

Hi, I'm Lucia and I recently graduated from college with a degree in graphic arts. I really like doing animation and would love to work in TV or film. However, during college, I got an internship where I designed a website for a furniture company. As soon as the internship ended, I sent out a lot of résumés listing my job experience. Then I got a job offer to work on the website for a department store. It isn't really the kind of work I want, but I did not get any other offers.

Lucia's online presence:

Lucia Martinez

Lucia shared an article:
5 Amazing Places to Visit

Lucia shared a photo:
cute animal pic

Lucia shared an article:
New Restaurant Opening Downtown

Lucia Martinez

Graphics Intern at Freedom Furniture Company

Last updated: 8 months ago

Lucia Martinez
Graphic Design

More work coming soon!

Lucia's mission statement:

"I have a degree in graphic design, and I love being creative and designing new things."

1 **What mistakes did Lucia make before she began her job search?**
- a Her brand and goals were not clear.
- b She did not talk to friends and family.
- c She included too much information.

2 **What problems do you see with Lucia's online presence?**
- a She looks too serious.
- b She has not updated her professional profile for a long time.
- c Her website does not reflect her goals.

3 **What problems do you see with Lucia's mission statement?**
- a She is not expressing what she wants to achieve.
- b It is too long and includes too many details.
- c It does not create a brand.

B PAIRS **Work together to write a new mission statement for Lucia.**

Step 5 Project

PAIRS In your online course, you asked friends and family to describe you, and then you wrote a mission statement. Share your notes and your mission statement with a partner. Give feedback on your partner's mission statement. Read the example.

I asked five people to describe me. More than one person said I was patient, kind, and friendly. That fits well with my mission statement, which is: I love to work with people. As a hospital nurse, I want to use my communication skills and medical knowledge to help patients heal and lead healthier lives.

Step 6 Talk!

PAIRS How important is personal branding to you? How important is personal branding to companies? Read the statistics and discuss. Are you surprised with the results? Why?

70% of companies search the online presence of job applicants before they hire them.

85% of companies decide to hire or not hire employees because of their online presence.

79% of companies rejected a job applicant based on their social media presence.

Step 7 Going forward

A PAIRS In your online course, you reflected on how you could develop or improve your personal brand. Discuss. Listen to the example.

B SHARE Present your ideas to the class.

VOCABULARY PRACTICE Go to page 81.

I can describe strategies for building my personal brand. ☐

11 MODULE

Job Search

What Is Networking?

DISCUSSION STRATEGIES

Go to page 68.

Step 1 Get started

A Refresh your memory! Watch the *What You'll Learn* video.

B Look at the photo. Why is a networking meeting like this useful? What advice do you have for someone who goes to a meeting like this?

C Check your understanding. Go to page 64.

Step 2 Tell your story

A THINK In your online course, you thought about who is in your network. When did you need help and how did they help you? Listen to the example.

B PAIRS Discuss your story.

C SHARE Tell your story to the class.

Step 3 Take away

THINK Complete the chart. Think about the questions. Then write your answers.

1 What kinds of information can you get from a professional network?	
2 Why is it important to meet people from your network in person?	
3 Why is it a good idea to meet with network contacts when you travel?	
4 Why is it important to help people in your network?	

Step 4 Activate your knowledge

A PAIRS Read the scenarios and think about each person's networking skills. Make a list of strengths and weaknesses.

1

Elena has always been active on social media, and she has hundreds of online friends. They include friends from school, family, co-workers, and old bosses. Most of Elena's posts are personal; photos of places she visits and information about her life. She does not see her online friends face-to-face, and she does not have any contact information for most of them. Now, Elena wants to make a career change, but she is not sure what to do.

Strengths	Weaknesses

2

Rafal is an engineer who would like to find work in a new city. He knows people who work in other places, but he is very busy so he does not stay in touch with them. Recently, he went out of town to a professional conference (a large meeting). There were engineers in his field from all over the world, and he went to a lot of interesting lectures. He enjoyed the conference and learned a lot. Every day, he attended lectures, ate his meals alone, and then went back to his hotel room to rest and do some work.

Strengths	Weaknesses

3

Pia works at a school in a small community. The school is trying to raise money for a student trip. She contacted business owners and other people in her network and asked them to give products or services for the school to sell. Pia asked friends to help at the sale, but she didn't advertise for more volunteers. The sale was successful, and all the money from the sale went to pay for the trip, but there were still many products in boxes at the end of the day because there weren't enough people to help sell them.

Strengths	Weaknesses

B PAIRS Discuss Elena's, Rafal's, and Pia's strengths and weaknesses. What advice would you give them for improving their networking skills?

C SHARE Present your ideas to the class.

Step 5 Project

A PAIRS In your online course, you researched professional groups and wrote about two that interest you and how you would use them. Share the information with a partner. Read the example.

I found two interesting groups related to a career in pharmacy. One of them is a local group of women in medicine. They mostly meet on social media to discuss experiences they're having at work, but they also meet in person once in a while. The other group is a national professional organization. It's a good place to learn about new things that are happening in the field, and they have a national conference every year where you can go to lectures and network.

B SHARE Tell the class about one of the groups that interests you.

Step 6 Talk!

How important is networking? What has been your experience with networking? Read the survey results about jobs and networks. Then discuss the questions.

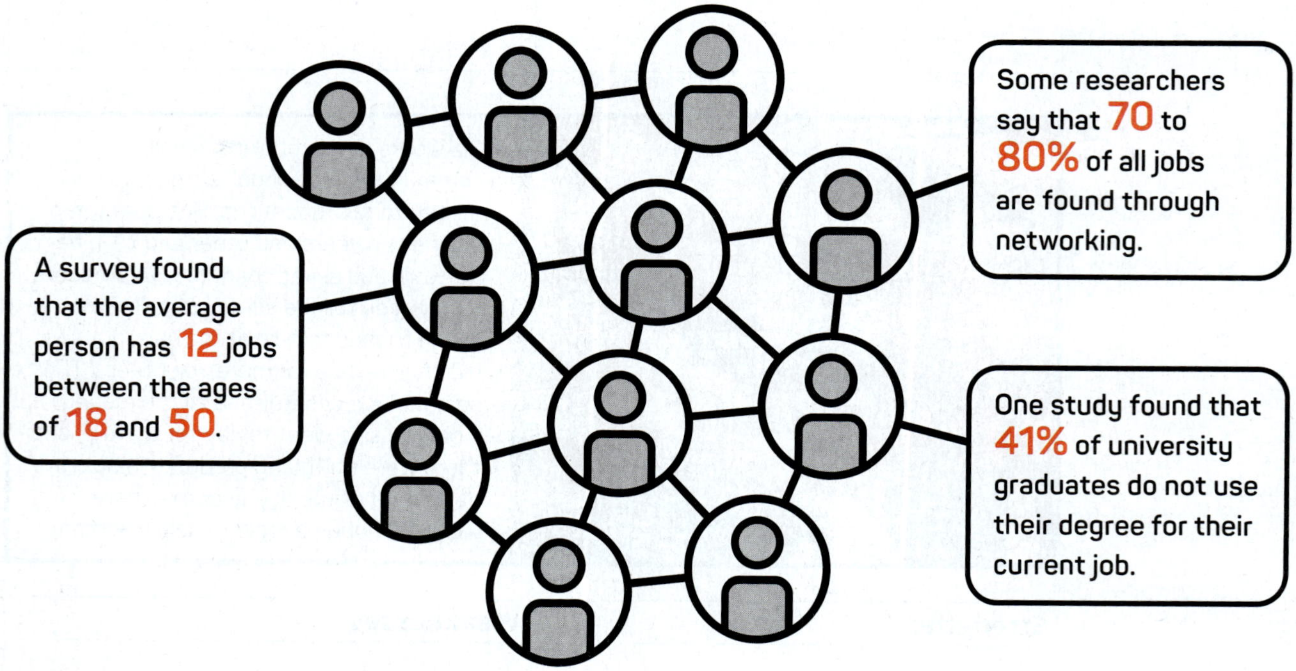

- How do these results compare to your own experience and the experiences of people you know?
- What does each result suggest about the importance of networking?

Step 7 Going forward

A PAIRS In your online course, you reflected on how you could improve your networking skills. Discuss. Listen to the example.

B SHARE Present your ideas to the class.

VOCABULARY PRACTICE
Go to page 82.

I can describe specific strategies for building and growing my professional network. ☐

MODULE 12

Interviewing

Interview Basics

DISCUSSION STRATEGIES
Go to page 68.

Step 1

Get started

A Refresh your memory! Watch the *What You'll Learn* video.

B Look at the photo. How do you think the person being interviewed feels? Why?

C Check your understanding. Go to page 65.

Step 2 Tell your story

A THINK In your online course, you thought about a past interview. Think about why it was or was not successful. Listen to the example.

B PAIRS Discuss your story.

C SHARE Tell your story to the class.

Step 3 Activate your knowledge

A THINK Look at the photos and read about people having job interviews. Then answer the questions.

1

Marco has an interview for an assistant position at an architecture company. He wants to prepare some questions to ask his interviewer. Put an X next to the questions Marco *should not* ask.

- ☐ What kind of constructions do you design at this company?
- ☐ What kind of projects would I be working on first?
- ☐ How many people work here?
- ☐ Will I get any training?
- ☐ What are the duties for this job?
- ☐ Will I be working in a large team or a small team?

2

Bora has a job interview next week, and she wants to be well-prepared. She calls the company and talks to a receptionist. Put an X next to the questions she *should not* ask.

- ☐ Is the interview at your location on Oak Street?
- ☐ Do you know who will interview me?
- ☐ Do you know how much that job pays?
- ☐ Do you like working there?
- ☐ My interview is at 3:00, right?
- ☐ Do you know what kind of person they're looking for?

3

Ken had an online interview. It went well in some ways, but not in others. Put an X next to the mistakes that Ken should have avoided in his interview.

- ☐ He practiced answers to common job interview questions.
- ☐ He did not know the company dress code, so he wore a T-shirt and jeans.
- ☐ He had to start a couple of minutes late because he was downloading the app.
- ☐ His mic was off at first, and his interviewers could not hear him.
- ☐ An interviewer asked for a list of references, and Ken said, "I can send that to you tomorrow."
- ☐ He was ready to talk about his strengths and weaknesses.

B PAIRS **Discuss your answers. What advice would you give these people for their next interview?**

Step 4 Take away

A THINK **Imagine that you are going to an in-person job interview next week. What things should and should you not do? Make a dos and don'ts list.**

Interview dos	Interview don'ts

B PAIRS **Discuss your lists with a partner. Make changes if necessary.**

Step 5 Project

A PAIRS **In your online course, you researched a company that you might like to work for. Talk about what you learned. Read the example.**

The company I researched was BootCorp. They make outdoor clothing, and they have stores in the United States, Europe, and South America. Their company values are all about taking care of the environment and being creative. Their stores seem like a great place to work. They have a lot of different kinds of job openings, but unfortunately none in my city right now. Their social media has information about their products, but they also link to a lot of articles about outdoor activities and the environment.

B SHARE **Tell the class about the most interesting company you researched.**

Step 6 Talk!

PAIRS Some people might do unusual things to get a new job. Read the excerpts and discuss the questions.

People Who Did Unusual Things to Get a Job

Interactive Video

One man made an interactive video résumé. Employers could watch him talk about himself and select links to see more information about his job experience and skills. He sent copies of the video to employers and then posted the video online.

Parental Help

A man went to a job interview for a technical position and his father decided to accompany him. The younger man did not speak much during the interview, but his father explained that he was a great employee. He also asked how much his son would be paid for the job.

Billboard

One young man applied for many jobs but did not get hired anywhere. He made a website with his résumé and portfolio, and then bought advertisements saying "Hire me!" with the web address. He even bought a large billboard with his face and web address on it.

- What do you think of each idea?
- Which people do you think got a job as a result?
- Do you know of any other people who did unusual things to get a job?

Step 7 Going forward

A PAIRS In your online course, you reflected on how you could improve your interviewing skills. Discuss. Listen to the example.

B SHARE Present your ideas to the class.

VOCABULARY PRACTICE
Go to page 83.

I can describe specific strategies for preparing for a job interview. ☐

CHECK YOUR UNDERSTANDING

Check your understanding 1

REFRESH YOUR MEMORY!

Review the Online Course material in your Resources.

Choose the best answers. More than one answer may be correct in some items.

1 You will be able to communicate more effectively if you think about ____.

- **a** how well you understand and like your audience
- **b** what you say and who you say it to
- **c** the way you communicate and how it is delivered

2 How can you communicate a clear message?

- **a** by using professional language and correct grammar
- **b** by sharing information in person and in writing
- **c** by including all of the necessary information

3 It is important to think about your audience. This can help you decide ____.

- **a** whether you should use polite speech
- **b** how formal your message should be
- **c** which medium they would prefer

4 Before you decide which medium to use, think about whether ____.

- **a** the message should be public or private
- **b** it is necessary to have a record of the message
- **c** your audience will understand your body language

5 You can deliver a message professionally by ____.

- **a** using a friendly tone and polite speech
- **b** using informal language to talk to your audience
- **c** using facial expressions that show interest in the conversation

6 Peter recently led a meeting and presented ideas to his team on how they could increase sales. He prepared a PowerPoint presentation, but some of the slides were very difficult to understand. After the meeting, the team was not sure what they should do to improve sales. What skill could have best prevented this communication breakdown?

- **a** Use professional language that is polite and accurate.
- **b** Think carefully about your message to deliver a clear message.
- **c** Decide if your medium should be public or private.

7 Elsa recently started a new job. She wanted to be friendly and get to know her manager, so she stopped by her desk to say hello and ask about her weekend. The manager was not pleased with this sudden visit. She asked Elsa to contact her beforehand if she wants to talk. What skill could have best prevented this communication breakdown?

- **a** Make sure that your message is accurate and free of errors.
- **b** Use body language and facial expressions to involve your audience.
- **c** Think about your audience to decide how formal to be.

8 The marketing manager asks Sophie to give him details about a new leadership skills course she has developed. He will use this information to create marketing materials about the course. Sophie sets up a call to share the details. The manager is not happy because there is a lot of information and he needs to be accurate. What skill could have best prevented this communication breakdown?

- **a** Think about whether you can see the audience's reactions to your message.
- **b** Decide what type of communication the audience prefers.
- **c** Use clear, complete sentences in formal spoken communication.

9 Pedro prepared a report of his company's finances over the past year. The report was complete and included useful information, but his manager found a few misspellings in it. His manager was not pleased and told Pedro he had to do better. What skill could have best prevented this communication breakdown?

- **a** Think about the audience and the details they need to know.
- **b** Decide what type of communication the audience prefers.
- **c** Deliver your message professionally.

Check your understanding 2

REFRESH YOUR MEMORY!

Review the Online Course material in your Resources.

Choose the best answers. More than one answer may be correct in some items.

1 **How can you improve your oral communication skills at work?**

a by thinking about how well and how much you listen
b by managing your emotions and using effective body language
c by encouraging others to express their feelings when they have a problem

2 **Good listeners ____.**

a interrupt when they do not understand something
b let people finish talking before adding their ideas
c confirm their understanding by asking questions

3 **Why should you try not to speak when you are upset at work?**

a because you may say something you will regret
b because it shows that you are an emotional person
c because other people are less likely to listen to you

4 **What should you include in an *I* message?**

a what the other person did wrong
b how you feel about a situation
c what you would like to see happen

5 **Why is it helpful to pay attention to other people's body language?**

a It shows how interested they are in the conversation.
b It shows when you might be talking too much.
c It shows when you should stand closer to them.

6 **Hannah is designing a house for a new client. The client is describing what she wants the house to look like. Hannah wants to make sure she understands her ideas. What should she do?**

a She should repeat back what she has heard.
b She should interrupt to add her own ideas.
c She should stay neutral when she does not like an idea.

7 **Julien manages a restaurant. He is meeting with Alex and Kate to share ideas on how to improve the customers' dining experience. He has been talking for a long time, and the meeting is almost over. Alex and Kate also want to make some suggestions. What should they do?**

a They should listen to what Julien has to say and wait until he has finished.
b They should stop Julien and tell him they have something important to add.
c They should look at their phone to check the time and show that time is running out.

8 **Layla is in a video meeting. She is listening to her co-worker explain how to use a new software program. The information her co-worker is presenting is not very clear. What should Layla say?**

a "You're not explaining the software clearly. Should we meet later to go over it?"
b "I'm sorry, but I'm confused. Can we go over it one more time?"
c "This isn't very clear. Can you explain the software better?"

9 **Galen is a real estate agent. He helps people buy and sell houses. He met with a client who wanted to sell her house. He thought the meeting went well, but she decided to work with a different agent. What might have gone wrong?**

a He continually made eye contact with her when she asked questions.
b He continually kept talking to show how much he was interested in working with her.
c He continually stopped the client while she was talking to describe how he could help her.

Check your understanding 3

REFRESH YOUR MEMORY!

Review the Online Course material in your Resources.

Choose the best answers. More than one answer may be correct in some items.

1 Setting SMART goals ____.

- **a** is connected to success
- **b** can improve your intelligence
- **c** helps you get where you want to go

2 What does it mean for a goal to be specific?

- **a** It means that the goal is measurable.
- **b** It means that the goal is detailed or exact.
- **c** It means that the goal gives general information.

3 A measurable goal includes ____.

- **a** how much work is needed to achieve it
- **b** the time frame needed to complete it
- **c** how important it is for you to achieve it

4 When a SMART goal is relevant, it is ____.

- **a** achievable within a time period
- **b** connected to your past goals
- **c** related to what you want to do

5 Why is it helpful for a SMART goal to be time-bound?

- **a** because it can motivate you to complete your goal
- **b** because it can make it easier for you to achieve your goal
- **c** because it can motivate you to set a difficult goal

6 **Zahra manages a team of five people. She is very busy and often forgets to check in with her team. Her goal is to improve her communication with her team members over the next month. How can Zahra make this goal more specific?**

- **a** by providing details about her busy schedule
- **b** by adding a time frame for completing this goal
- **c** by stating that she will meet with each person weekly

7 **Li works at the front desk of a hotel. Customers who are happy with her service give her positive reviews. The more reviews she receives, the faster she can be promoted. Her goal is to get a large number of positive reviews by the end of the year. How can Li make this goal measurable?**

- **a** by adding a deadline for achieving a high number
- **b** by adding a specific number that she wants to achieve
- **c** by describing how she will get a high number

8 **Jakob designs online courses for a university. It takes three months to design and develop a new course, but his goal is to design the next course in two weeks because he does not have much time. How can Jakob make this goal more achievable?**

- **a** by giving himself a more realistic time frame
- **b** by working during the day and at night
- **c** by staying positive and believing in himself

9 **Oliver is a receptionist at a busy medical clinic. He schedules patient appointments and manages patient records. Sometimes it takes him two days to return patients' phone calls. He needs to manage his time better. What goal is relevant to helping Oliver get more done?**

- **a** Set a goal to meet with ten more patients every day.
- **b** Set a goal to take ten minutes to file patients' records every day.
- **c** Set a goal to call at least ten more patients every day.

10 **Lucia wants to open her own business. She is working on her business plan. Her goal is to figure out how much it will cost to run the business. How can Lucia's goal be improved?**

- **a** by making it achievable
- **b** by making it relevant
- **c** by making it time-bound

Check your understanding 4

REFRESH YOUR MEMORY!

Review the Online Course material in your Resources.

Choose the best answers. More than one answer may be correct in some items.

1 **How can you benefit from learning to work on a team?**

- **a** You will get better at talking to people.
- **b** You will make more friends.
- **c** You will discover different ways of doing things.

2 **Good team members ____.**

- **a** like to work independently
- **b** put the shared goal first
- **c** rely on each other

3 **To be a good team member you need to ____.**

- **a** care about what your teammates say
- **b** share ideas and solve problems together
- **c** communicate only when you have a problem

4 **When team members are kind and respectful, they ____.**

- **a** explain why their opinion is the best
- **b** try to come to an agreement
- **c** encourage others to share ideas

5 **Darya and her co-workers are putting together a report about how their organization helps the community. One of her colleagues has not started writing his part of the report, and it needs to be finished in two days. Darya is worried about getting the report done on time. What skills are missing from this team?**

- **a** Not everyone is responsible and doing their part.
- **b** Not everyone knows their role.
- **c** Not everyone is kind and respectful.

6 **Hajun works with a team of five people. A new project manager recently joined the team. The new manager wants the team to check in with each other every morning for fifteen minutes. Hajun and his teammates do not understand why this is necessary. The team feels they work well together and communicate with each other when needed. How could this team be improved?**

- **a** They could skip the morning meeting and communicate when needed.
- **b** The project manager could encourage the team to use their skills.
- **c** They could be open to different ways of working.

7 **A team had a great experience developing a marketing plan for a new client. They each worked on an area of the plan that they are skilled at. Yvonne identified the marketing goals. Patrick outlined the details. Maureen measured the plan's success. The client was very happy with their work. What teamwork skill helped this team the most?**

- **a** being kind and respectful to each other
- **b** knowing their strengths
- **c** being flexible

8 **Mauricio notices that his team has been making mistakes. He is not sure why this is happening. He spoke to some of the team members a couple of weeks ago, and they seemed to be doing fine. He wonders if they could be rushing to meet the deadline and that is causing the mistakes. How can this team be improved?**

- **a** Mauricio could have regular team meetings so that everyone can check in.
- **b** Mauricio could encourage team members to keep their eye on the goal.
- **c** The team could be more responsible by completing their work on time.

Check your understanding 5

REFRESH YOUR MEMORY!

Review the Online Course material in your Resources.

Choose the best answers. More than one answer may be correct in some items.

1 Critical thinking is a set of skills you use to analyze and evaluate ____.

- **a** feelings and emotions
- **b** personal experiences
- **c** different viewpoints

2 Your analysis of the information you have gathered will help you ____.

- **a** make an informed decision
- **b** review more sources
- **c** listen to others

3 Gathering information from different sources ____.

- **a** is the most difficult step in the critical thinking process
- **b** can help you understand an issue from different viewpoints
- **c** is needed when you claim something is true

4 When analyzing and evaluating evidence, you should ____.

- **a** think about whether it comes from a respected source
- **b** decide if it is based on facts or opinions
- **c** trust the source because most sources are honest

5 If you find new or better information at the end of the critical thinking process, you may need to ____.

- **a** keep evaluating and analyzing evidence
- **b** ask people their opinions about the issue
- **c** change your mind about the issue

6 Ying is a healthcare administrator at a hospital. Many patients do not have a good opinion about their experience at the hospital. As a result, Ying wants to improve patient care. What is the first thing she should do?

- **a** Look at evidence carefully.
- **b** Gather information from different sources.
- **c** Review her critical thinking process.

7 Doug owns a small tech company. He is looking for ways to lower company costs. He reviews different cost-cutting strategies and asks his employees for their viewpoints. Many of them think he should close the office space and allow employees to work from home. This would save the company a lot of money. Other companies he looked at have done this, too. However, Doug does not like this idea, so he decides that there must be a better solution. What step is missing from Doug's critical thinking process?

- **a** Gather information from different viewpoints.
- **b** Think about the source of information.
- **c** Think about information with an open mind.

8 Felipe needs to buy new chairs for everyone in the office. He found a chair online that had many positive customer reviews and a good price. When he asked his co-workers for their opinion about the chair, one person said that it did not look comfortable. Based on this viewpoint, Felipe quickly decided not to buy the chairs. How could Felipe improve his critical thinking?

- **a** by listening to people's feelings and beliefs
- **b** by looking at the evidence more carefully
- **c** by separating facts from opinions

9 Stephanie and Anatoly want to remodel their kitchen. They are meeting with a designer to decide what changes they will make to the space. They have looked at photos of different kitchens and design plans. They still cannot make a decision. What should they do?

- **a** They should think more about the source of information.
- **b** They should ask the designer to make a decision for them.
- **c** They should look at more designs and continue to evaluate.

Check your understanding 6

REFRESH YOUR MEMORY!

Review the Online Course material in your Resources.

Choose the best answers. More than one answer may be correct in some items.

1 **What are some of the qualities of a good leader?**
- **a** They give positive instead of negative feedback.
- **b** They take responsibility and make decisions.
- **c** They have good ideas and inspire others.

2 **Good leaders ____.**
- **a** ask others to listen carefully and respect everyone
- **b** work well with others and are trustworthy
- **c** give feedback and are brave enough to accept it

3 **____ is the very best way to learn to lead.**
- **a** A leadership skills course
- **b** Watching a leader
- **c** Experience

4 **What are some ways you can improve your leadership skills?**
- **a** by learning from famous leaders you respect
- **b** by trying to solve problems the same way
- **c** by taking risks and learning from your mistakes

5 **Why is it important for leaders to stay motivated?**
- **a** because it can help them accept difficult feedback
- **b** because it can make them more outgoing
- **c** because it can motivate others

6 **Hija is a marketing director for a soft drink company. A new product is not selling very well. Her team needs to come up with a new marketing plan. She listens closely to her team's ideas and looks for opportunities to market the product in new ways. Which leadership skills does Hija use in this situation?**
- **a** She gives helpful feedback.
- **b** She inspires others to think of good ideas.
- **c** She is open to innovative solutions.

7 **Marcel is meeting with his staff to share changes he will make to the company. One person asks a question that Marcel is not able to answer. He admits that he does not know the answer and will respond with more information soon. What leadership skill does Marcel use in this situation?**
- **a** He motivates staff to do a good job.
- **b** He values the work everyone does.
- **c** He acts honestly and respectfully.

8 **Kaito works for Event Planners, Inc. He leads a team that organizes an educational conference each year. Hundreds of teachers and school administrators attend the conference to learn about new educational products. Two days before the conference is supposed to begin, Kaito learns that the main speaker may not be able to attend. Which leadership skills should he use to improve this situation?**
- **a** He should keep a positive attitude and hope that the speaker is able to attend.
- **b** He should have a can-do attitude and take positive action to solve the problem.
- **c** He should focus on his other responsibilities and inspiring others.

Check your understanding 7

REFRESH YOUR MEMORY!

Review the Online Course material in your Resources.

Choose the best answers. More than one answer may be correct in some items.

1 Time management tools can help you manage your ____.

a stress
b ideas
c workload

2 Good planners use these time management tools to write down meetings and tasks to help them meet deadlines.

a daily diary
b calendar
c to-do list

3 When you use backward planning, you start planning from the ____ and work backward.

a due date
b most important task
c least important task

4 Why is it helpful to rank tasks using an ABC grid?

a It can help you stay on track.
b It can help you finish all of your tasks within a day or two.
c It can help you finish the most important tasks first.

5 Tomas just started a new job as an office administrator. He has weekly projects and meetings. He also has many daily tasks. He is having a difficult time getting everything done on time. What should he do?

a He should categorize tasks using backward planning.
b He should use a calendar to keep track of his work.
c He should put off easy projects until the last minute.

6 Himari is a software engineer. He manages his workload by first adding important project deadlines to his calendar in red. He then writes down the steps for completing these projects on his calendar in blue. Which time management tool does Himari use?

a backward planning
b a to-do list
c an ABC grid

7 Susanne is a construction manager. She creates building schedules and makes sure projects stay on track. Every morning, she likes to write down the tasks she needs to get done for the day. Which time management tool does Susanne use?

a backward planning
b a to-do list
c an ABC grid

8 Ahmad is opening a restaurant in two weeks. He still has a lot to do to get the restaurant ready. He has categorized the tasks he needs to get done. Tasks in the first category must be completed right away. The second category tasks should be completed by the end of the week. The tasks in the last category can be put off until next week. Which time management tool is Ahmad using?

a backward planning
b a to-do list
c an ABC grid

Check your understanding 8

REFRESH YOUR MEMORY!

Review the Online Course material in your Resources.

Choose the best answers. More than one answer may be correct in some items.

1 **Why is it important to have healthy habits?**

a They can help you sleep less.
b They can help you think clearly.
c They can help you have more energy.

2 **What are some healthy habits?**

a drinking two or three alcoholic drinks per day
b drinking about 2.7–3.7 liters of water per day
c eating lean protein, low-fat dairy, and whole grains

3 **What are some unhealthy habits?**

a exercising at night before going to bed
b drinking alcohol in moderation
c being around secondhand smoke

4 **Unhealthy habits can cause ____.**

a heart disease and cancer
b accidents and injuries
c more smoking and drinking

5 **Vincent owns a landscaping business. He spends a lot of time doing physical work outside. When it is hot, he does not feel well and cannot work as well. What should Vincent do to work better in the heat?**

a practice yoga
b get enough sleep
c drink enough water

6 **Yalina eats breakfast every day before going to work. She usually has a piece of toast with butter and jam. She exercises three times per week for an hour. She enjoys having a couple of beers with dinner and a cigarette after her meal. She recently learned that she has high blood pressure and is in danger of getting diabetes. How should Yalina change her habits to improve her health?**

a She should eat a balanced breakfast.
b She should drink less alcohol.
c She should try electronic cigarettes.

7 **Luis recently started a job as a computer programmer. He sits at a desk for most of the day. Lately, he has been gaining weight. What healthy habit would help Luis control his weight?**

a aerobic exercise
b tobacco products
c strength training

8 **Naomi does not get a lot of sleep. The city lights keep her awake. She also skips breakfast often so that she is not late for work. She feels tired all day long. What can Naomi do to sleep better and improve her energy at work?**

a She can have 2–3 glasses of wine at night to help her sleep.
b She can use curtains to make her room darker.
c She can eat a balanced breakfast.

Check your understanding 9

REFRESH YOUR MEMORY!

Review the Online Course material in your Resources.

Choose the best answers. More than one answer may be correct in some items.

1 **Social responsibility means that we are interested in ways to ____.**

a make people's lives better

b improve our work skills

c reach our goals

2 **What are some examples of personal social responsibility?**

a taking a leadership course

b cleaning up a local park

c giving food to the homeless

3 **Why is it important to practice good workplace etiquette?**

a It will help you learn new skills.

b It can help you get a promotion.

c It will make others want to work with you.

4 **What are some ways to practice good etiquette at work?**

a Follow workplace culture.

b Arrive early, and don't rush out.

c Avoid using digital communication tools.

5 **Why should you avoid using your personal phone at work?**

a because it can make you less productive

b because it can harm your relationships with friends

c because it can disturb people around you

6 **Bora recently started a new job as a public affairs specialist. She wants to get to know her co-workers better. She has tried to have informal conversations with people before meetings, but they seem to feel uncomfortable around her. Bora is not sure what she is doing wrong. Which etiquette tip does Bora need to follow?**

a Do not complain too much.

b Pay attention to how people communicate.

c Treat virtual meetings like in-person meetings.

7 **Danilo is a medical assistant at a busy clinic. He does not like it when patients talk so much that he has to spend more time than usual with them. He is always telling the doctors that he thinks these patients are annoying. The doctors have asked him to stop sharing his negative opinions about patients. Which etiquette tip does Danilo need to follow?**

a Follow workplace culture.

b Don't complain too much.

c Keep text interactions professional.

8 **Zoe works at an international company where employees use a chat tool to communicate with each other in real-time. One of Zoe's co-workers had a problem with a message that Zoe sent because it contained several emojis. Emojis are not used at their office because they are too informal and can be confusing. Which etiquette tip does Zoe need to follow?**

a Keep text interactions professional.

b Put away your phone.

c Do not complain too much.

9 **Anders has been working from his home office. He and his team have scheduled weekly online meetings. He is always online on time and comes prepared. While others are talking, he often turns off his camera and mutes his microphone in order to make coffee or go get something to eat. His teammates seem upset when they can no longer see or hear him. Which etiquette tip does Anders need to follow?**

a Pay attention to how people communicate.

b Arrive early, and do not rush out.

c Treat virtual meetings like in-person meetings.

Check your understanding 10

REFRESH YOUR MEMORY!

Review the Online Course material in your Resources.

Choose the best answers. More than one answer may be correct in some items.

1 What qualities should be highlighted in a personal brand?

- **a** skills and experiences
- **b** strengths and weaknesses
- **c** personality and attitudes

2 How can you start building your personal brand?

- **a** Create a logo that emphasizes your strengths.
- **b** Think about what would make people notice you.
- **c** Ask others to describe you in a few words.

3 Once you know your brand, you should ____.

- **a** match your brand to your long-term goals
- **b** highlight qualities that will impress your audience
- **c** spend six months thinking about your goals

4 A mission statement describes ____.

- **a** your past work experience and qualifications
- **b** what you want to achieve
- **c** the qualities that will help you meet your goals

5 What are some ways to develop your brand?

- **a** Highlight it in your résumé and cover letter.
- **b** Create a special brand for your online presence.
- **c** Practice presenting your brand to new people.

6 How can you continue to develop your brand as you grow and change?

- **a** Think about how others describe you.
- **b** Revise your goals as needed.
- **c** Compare your brand to other people's.

7 Jeong-ho wants to change careers. He has started applying for jobs in project management. He thought about his career goals and asked his friends to describe his strengths. Then he revised his résumé and cover letter so that they reflect his new goals. His professional social media account includes his work experience and his mission statement from several years ago. What mistake did Jeong-ho make?

- **a** He did not revise his goals.
- **b** He did not think about his online presence.
- **c** He did not talk to his friends before developing his brand.

8 Jamila wants to apply for a management position at the customer service department where she works. She made sure to highlight her strong communication and problem-solving skills on her résumé, cover letter, and social media account. She knows these qualities are important to employers. People also think she is patient and has a positive attitude. Unfortunately, she did not show this in her brand because she did not think of it. What mistake did Jamila make?

- **a** She did not think about her audience when developing her brand.
- **b** She did not talk to her co-workers before developing her brand.
- **c** She did not think about her online presence.

9 Arjun wants to be a financial planner at a large corporation. He knows his mission statement needs to describe what is important to him, what he wants to achieve, and the qualities that will help him. Choose the best mission statement for him.

- **a** My goal is to help clients meet their financial goals by using my strong data analysis skills to provide financial advice.
- **b** I have over five years of experience working in finance for a small company. My goal is to work somewhere where I will have opportunities for promotion.
- **c** I have many years of experience helping staff keep track of their finances. I am reliable and honest. Clients are happy with my work.

10 Rosa recently received a degree in civil engineering. She is applying for several civil engineering positions. She knows her mission statement needs to describe what is important to her, what she wants to achieve, and the qualities that will help her. Choose the best mission statement.

- **a** I have a Bachelor's Degree in Civil Engineering. I am skilled at mathematics, building and construction design, and engineering design.
- **b** I am skilled at using design software, like AutoCAD. I also enjoyed leading difficult projects and worked well with others in my undergraduate courses.
- **c** My goal is to use my design and project management skills to construct buildings that are beautiful and environmentally friendly.

Check your understanding 11

REFRESH YOUR MEMORY!

Review the Online Course material in your Resources.

Choose the best answers. More than one answer may be correct in some items.

1 **You should relate to your professional network ____.**
- **a** separately from your social network
- **b** the same way as your social network
- **c** in a more formal way than your social network

2 **Your professional network can ____.**
- **a** make sure you receive a promotion or get hired for a job
- **b** keep you updated on important issues in your industry
- **c** help you find out about training or job opportunities

3 **You can build your professional network by ____.**
- **a** waiting for people to introduce themselves to you at a conference
- **b** looking for places online where people in your field meet to discuss issues
- **c** sharing your contact information with new people you meet

4 **How can you maintain your professional network?**
- **a** Organize small get-togethers with contacts who know each other.
- **b** Offer to help others and thank people who have helped you.
- **c** Send updates about your work life to your contacts everyday.

5 **Manuel recently started his career as a software engineer. He is at a technology conference, but he does not know anyone there. What should he do?**
- **a** Introduce himself and get people's contact information.
- **b** Share details about job opportunities with his network.
- **c** Ask his professional network about training opportunities.

6 **Mei-ling met a colleague for coffee. She and her colleague both work in marketing, but her colleague is not happy at her current job because her co-workers are not very helpful and the work is not interesting. What networking strategy should Mei-ling use to help her colleague?**
- **a** Thank her colleague on social media for meeting with her.
- **b** Remove her colleague's co-workers from her list of contacts.
- **c** Share information about job openings at her company.

7 **Alexander is attending a conference in Toronto. He will be busy during the day, but his evenings are free. What should he do next to maintain his network?**
- **a** Look through his list of contacts who live in the city and suggest meeting up.
- **b** Ask his contacts about training opportunities.
- **c** Share an interesting article with his list of contacts.

8 **Parvati attended a professional event where she met many people in her field. She left her phone at home, so she had to write down people's names and emails in her notebook. What should she do next to build her network?**
- **a** Mention the professional event in a social media post when she gets home.
- **b** Enter the contact information into an app and organize it.
- **c** Chat online with the people she met.

Check your understanding 12

REFRESH YOUR MEMORY!

Review the Online Course material in your Resources.

Choose the best answers. More than one answer may be correct in some items.

1 **What are some ways that you can research a company before your interview?**

- **a** Study their website's "About us" page to learn about their goals, products, and services.
- **b** Check your interviewers' social media accounts to help you learn more about them.
- **c** Prepare a list of questions you would like to ask your interviewers about the company.

2 **It is important to learn more about your interview ahead of time. Which of the following questions are okay to ask a company before your interview?**

- **a** Can you tell me more about the job requirements and duties?
- **b** Will I be meeting with a group of interviewers at the same time?
- **c** What are the names and positions of the interviewers?

3 **What are some ways you can plan to make a good first impression at an in-person interview?**

- **a** Choose clothes that follow the company's dress code.
- **b** Arrive on time, not early or late.
- **c** Map out the route ahead of time.

4 **Why is it important to bring documents with you to an interview?**

- **a** It can make you look organized and feel more confident.
- **b** An interviewer may ask to see a few of your work samples.
- **c** Most interviewers will require you to share your business card with them.

5 **You should ____ when you practice for an online interview.**

- **a** use the same software while answering questions
- **b** answer popular interview questions to yourself
- **c** practice with friends and encourage them to ask follow-up questions

6 **Monique is interviewing for an office assistant position. What should she bring with her to the interview to show that she is prepared and organized?**

- **a** references with contact numbers
- **b** articles about the company
- **c** copies of her résumé

7 **Ming has applied for a position as sales associate at a large home improvement company. He has studied the company's website to get ready for his interview. However, he wants to learn more about how they relate to customers. How should he research this information?**

- **a** by searching the internet for information about the job duties and requirements
- **b** by checking the company's social media accounts to learn more about their values
- **c** by calling customer service and asking a representative about the company

8 **Alina has an interview with an online retail company. She wants to learn more about their interview process, but she cannot call to find out this information. The company already emailed her the interview time and place, and they specifically asked her not to call in advance. What can she do to learn more about the interview?**

- **a** Search the internet to see what people have shared about their interview experiences.
- **b** Email the company to ask if they can describe the interview process.
- **c** Ask her network if they have experience interviewing at this company.

9 **Samir has an interview for a hotel manager position. He is not sure what to wear because he cannot find the company's dress code. In the pictures on the company website, all the employees are dressed in formal clothes. What should he wear for the in-person job interview?**

- **a** new black jeans and a white T-shirt
- **b** a suit and tie
- **c** comfortable pants and a button-down shirt

10 **Paul has an interview for a software engineer position at a tech company. He is preparing a list of common interview questions to practice answering with a friend. Which questions should be included?**

- **a** Where was your last job located?
- **b** Why do you want to work here?
- **c** How have you solved a problem at work?

DISCUSSION STRATEGIES

Discussion strategies

When you are in class or at work, you may need to take part in discussions. To successfully participate, you can use a number of different kinds of strategies. They include strategies that help you:

1 Work with others
2 Clarify what you hear or clarify what you say
3 Get and stay involved in the discussion
4 Organize your ideas

During each discussion in class, choose one kind of strategy you want to improve or one you think will be useful. Pick a phrase and try to use it during the in-class activities. Remember to always say the phrase in a polite way.

You can listen to the phrases and examples ▶.

1 Working with others

Some strategies can make it easier to work with other people who are part of the discussion. If you can, try starting the discussion or helping to keep the discussion moving in the right direction. These strategies can help.

Management strategies	Sample phrases
a Starting the discussion	▶ Are we ready to start? ▶ Let's begin.
b Asking others to participate	▶ Who wants to answer first? ▶ Does anyone have anything to add?
c Helping specific people to get involved	▶ Chris, what do you think? ▶ Donna, do you have anything to add?
d Jumping in with talkative people	▶ That's a good point, but let's hear from other people. ▶ Let's hear what everyone else has to say.
e Staying on the topic	▶ That's interesting, but it's a different topic. ▶ We need to stay on topic.
f Keeping the discussion moving	▶ Let's move to the next question. ▶ We can talk about that later.
g Telling someone you can't hear them*	▶ I'm sorry. I didn't hear what you said. ▶ Can you speak a little louder?
h Telling someone they speak too fast*	▶ I'm sorry. Can you say that a little slower? ▶ Can you speak more slowly, please?

*You can also use clarification strategies to make sure you understood someone who is quiet or talks too quickly.

2 Clarifying

Sometimes it is hard for you to understand what someone is saying or for others to understand you. Clarifying is a natural part of discussions. Even native speakers use these strategies because not everyone understands everything all the time!

Clarification strategies	Sample phrases	Examples
a Clarifying (when you didn't understand someone else)	▶ I don't understand. ▶ I'm not sure what you mean.	

Discussion strategies

Clarification strategies	Sample phrases	Examples
b Restating (when someone doesn't understand you)	In other words . . .	A: People remember you if you have a strong personal brand. B: I'm sorry. I don't understand. A: In other words, a strong personal brand helps people remember you.
	I mean . . .	A: A habit is something we do often and it doesn't require us to think about it before we do it. B: Sorry? A: I mean, a habit is something you do all the time and you don't have to think about it.
c Checking (when you want to make sure someone understands you)	Just checking—do you see what I mean? Is that clear? Do you have any questions?	
d Paraphrasing (what the speaker says)	Are you saying that . . .	A: This new software will be more efficient. B: Are you saying that it's faster and easier to use than our current system?
	Do you mean that . . .	A: My team has way too many new projects. B: Do you mean that workload is a problem?
e Paraphrasing (what someone else says)	Lu said that . . . What . . . means is . . .	Lu said that clients have complained. What Kim means is he didn't set any SMART goals.

3 Getting involved

It can be challenging to participate in discussions. Sometimes you have to involve yourself without being asked, keep your turn (if others try to interrupt you), interrupt (when others are talking), and get your turn back (after being interrupted).

Participation strategies	Sample phrases	Examples
a Getting involved	Can I ask a question? I have something I'd like to say.	
b Keeping your turn	Excuse me, I'd just like to finish what I'm saying. I'm just about to finish.	
c Interrupting	Excuse me . . . Sorry to interrupt . . .	Excuse me, but I'd like to add something. Sorry to interrupt, but I have a question.
d Getting your turn back	As I was saying . . .	As I was saying, good leaders are willing to make decisions.
	Going back to what I was saying . . .	Going back to what I was saying, good leaders can motivate their team.
e Commenting (on what someone has said)	That's a good point . . . I see what you mean . . .	That's a good point, Kate. I see what you mean, Sam.
f Adding (to what someone has said)	I agree with you . . . and also . . .	I agree with you, Mia, and also, we need to improve time management.
	Another thing to consider is . . .	Yes, and another thing to consider is productivity.

Discussion strategies

4 Organizing

Lastly, organization techniques can help communication and make discussion easier to follow.

Organization techniques	Sample words and phrases	Examples
a Chronological	First . . . second . . . third . . . Next . . . then . . . later	▶ First, let's talk about the scenario. Second, let's share our ideas. Third, let's suggest ideas. ▶ Next, we will talk about some ideas for this proposal. Then, we'll work on it as a team. Later, we'll get together and share our work.
b Cause and effect	If . . . , then . . . When . . . then . . .	▶ If you use SMART goals, then you're more likely to succeed. ▶ When you check off an item on your to-do list, then you feel good about yourself.
c Categorical	There are three categories . . . The main characteristics . . .	▶ There are three categories of users for this technology: beginner, intermediate, and expert. ▶ These are the main characteristics that make someone a good leader.
d Problem and solution	The main problem is . . . One big issue is . . . The best solution is . . . We could . . .	▶ The main problem is that we don't have regular project meetings. ▶ One big issue is that we don't have enough resources for this project. ▶ The best solution is to form teams so that we get more ideas. ▶ We could work out a plan together as a team.
e Adding an idea	Also . . . In the same way . . .	▶ Networking sites are good places to look for jobs. Also, you can use those sites to meet people from other companies. ▶ Our physical health is important. In the same way, emotional wellness is essential for a balanced lifestyle.
f Contrast	Although . . . However . . .	▶ Although working in teams is important, being able to work independently is a valuable skill. ▶ She doesn't have a lot of experience in this industry. However, she was great in the interview.

VOCABULARY PRACTICE

Vocabulary practice 1

Exercise A

Complete the puzzle.

Across

2 to do something because of something that has happened
3 to cause a change in somebody or something
5 the way someone's face looks, often showing their feelings
8 small pieces of information about something
9 acting in a serious and correct way
10 information put in writing to save the facts for the future
11 to enter into a situation where you are not wanted

Down

1 the feeling that you like or want one thing more than another
3 correct, true, free from mistakes
4 free from worry about rules or ideas about being serious
6 the opinion you have of someone or something after seeing them or learning about them
7 a situation where something has failed or stopped working

Exercise B

Use 8 words or phrases from the puzzle to complete an employee's email to a co-worker.

Email

Jennifer Lee
To: Lisa Dayton
Subject: Morning meeting

Hey L,

You missed a serious meeting with Ms. M! I'll give you all the 1 ____________ when I see you. It looks like things went wrong after a(n) 2 ____________ in communication on one of the teams. It might 3 ____________ a relationship with a client—I'm not sure. Ms. M tried not to sound angry, but we all knew from her 4 ____________ that she really was not happy. She asked Chris to take notes, so everybody will get an official 5 ____________ of what she said. The main idea is, we have to do better with communication in the future, especially to make the right 6 ____________ on clients. I should probably try to be more 7 ____________. I like to be friendly and relaxed with people, but sometimes being 8 ____________ means I don't seem serious enough.

Let's talk soon!

Vocabulary practice 2

Exercise A

Complete the puzzle.

Across

2 Unhappy or angry about something that has happened: *I can't talk when I'm ____________.*

4 Not supporting any side when people or groups disagree: *Stay ____________; don't show support for either of them.*

6 A problem caused when you don't understand a situation or communication: *a small ____________ between team members*

8 To talk so you stop another person who was talking: *Please don't ____________!*

10 To say or think someone caused something bad to happen: *Don't ____________ me for your mistake!*

11 To show feelings or tell ideas: *____________ an opinion*

12 To stop feeling angry: *try to ____________*

Down

1 To check that something is correct or true: *Let's ____________ the time of the flight.*

3 Strong feelings: *her ____________ were clear from the look on her face*

5 To watch or listen carefully: *____________ to everything he says*

7 Taking part in something: *____________ in an interesting project*

9 To reply or answer: *____________ to an email*

Exercise B

Use 8 words or phrases from the puzzle to complete the conversations.

1

Do your co-workers ever 1 ____________ when you're talking?

Yes! And I get very 2 ____________ when they do that.

2

I hear that you 3 ____________ me for the problem.

What? No, I don't! There must be a 4 ____________.

3

I tried to 5 ____________ my questions clearly in my email to them. I hope they understand.

Well, you'll know if they understood when they 6 ____________.

4

You need to 7 ____________ before you say anything more.

OK, OK! But it's hard to manage my 8 ____________ in a situation like this!

Vocabulary practice 3

Exercise (A)

Read the clues and find the words and phrases.

A	H	W	K	J	Y	X	D	I	R	E	C	T	L	Y
P	S	E	T	A	S	I	D	E	B	Q	H	U	N	R
O	C	V	Y	E	Z	T	I	M	E	F	R	A	M	E
S	O	A	O	X	U	I	O	P	L	I	K	O	M	L
S	N	C	N	P	P	L	W	V	A	G	J	R	O	A
I	C	H	A	R	O	J	E	A	L	U	S	I	T	T
B	E	I	V	E	S	N	X	C	F	R	E	G	I	E
I	N	E	E	S	I	Z	A	H	D	E	N	I	V	D
L	T	V	R	S	T	V	C	R	S	O	M	N	A	W
I	R	E	A	L	I	S	T	I	C	U	R	A	T	L
T	A	V	G	I	V	P	L	E	K	T	K	L	E	J
Y	T	A	E	D	E	K	Y	O	X	Z	Y	A	N	E
A	E	R	Z	M	F	D	E	T	A	I	L	E	D	S
Y	I	N	B	O	X	E	A	C	T	U	A	L	L	Y
S	I	D	E	E	F	F	E	C	T	S	R	Z	I	O

1 If a medicine makes you feel bad, you may be experiencing these.
2 If you agree to do a job in a period of time, then you have agreed on this.
3 If you need to think very carefully about what you're doing, you must do this.
4 If you do this with money, then you'll have some later when you need it.
5 If you can do this to a math problem, then you will have the answer.
6 If there is a connection between two things, then this word describes them.
7 If your goal is really possible, then this word describes it.
8 If you give a report that is full of information, then this word describes it.
9 If your doctor gives you this kind of report on your health, that's good news.
10 If you change Plan A for Plan B, then this word describes Plan A.
11 If a situation is usual or normal, you can say it happens like this.
12 If you do something this way, you do it with no mistakes or changes at all.
13 If two things are connected this way, there's nothing else between them.
14 If something is really true (but might be surprising), you may want to use this word.

Exercise (B)

Use 7 words or phrases from the puzzle to complete Martin's email to a friend.

Email

Martin Chavez
To: Ali Samir
Subject: Job opening

Hi Ali,

Thanks for the message about a possible job at your company. I'm really interested. You always say **1** ____________ things about your co-workers, so it sounds like a good place to work. But you didn't tell me much about the job, so I have some questions.

- What **2** ____________ is the job? Your message about it wasn't very **3** ____________.
- How soon do they want somebody to start? What's the **4** ____________?
- I know your hours change from week to week. Can you tell me about how many hours I'd be working **5** ____________?
- You know I don't have a lot of work experience. Do you think I have a **6** ____________ chance of getting this job?

Maybe you could give me a call. If we could talk about the job, that would help me **7** ____________ what to do.

Thanks again!

Vocabulary practice 4

Exercise A

Complete the puzzle. What is the vertical word?

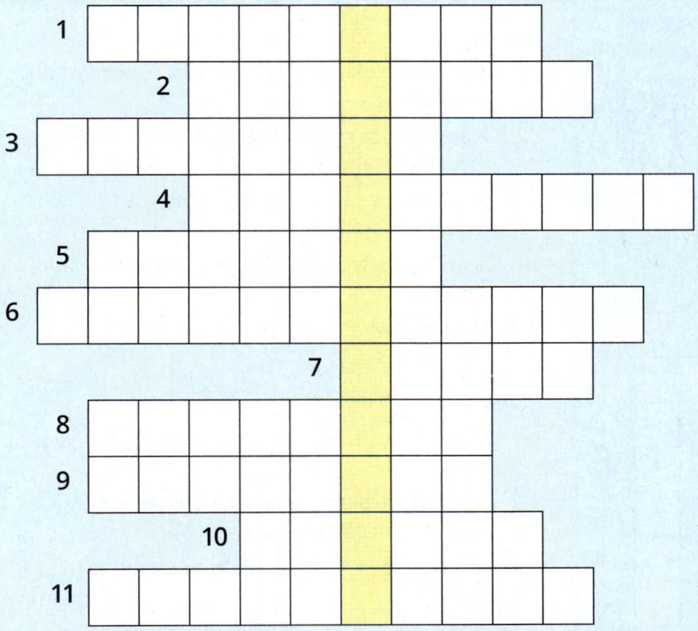

1 I like discussing things with my team at work. We ______ each other to share ideas.
2 Paul writes very well. That's a(n) ______ he brings to our team.
3 Sometimes I talk before I think. That's probably my biggest ______.
4 My team members really help when there's a problem. They're very ______.
5 I don't have a(n) ______ on that because I don't know anything about it.
6 I like all my teammates. They're easy to ______.
7 We're having a problem. I hope you can help us ______ it.
8 The people on that team often disagree. It seems there's a new ______ every day!
9 You can't always have everything go your way. We're a team. We all have to be ______.
10 Anna always does what she says she'll do. You can ______ her.
11 You're very quiet in team meetings. Why don't you take a more ______?

Exercise B

Use 7 words from the puzzle to complete the statements. Then choose your answers.

Are *YOU* a good team player at work? Take this quiz!

	Always	Sometimes	Never
1 I take a(n) ______ on my team.	☐	☐	☐
2 I have good relationships with my teammates. I ______ everyone.	☐	☐	☐
3 I ______ my teammates to share their ideas and opinions.	☐	☐	☐
4 My teammates can rely on me. I'm very ______.	☐	☐	☐
5 When there is a(n) ______ in my team, I work with others to solve the problem.	☐	☐	☐
6 I know how to be flexible. That is a(n) ______ I bring to my team.	☐	☐	☐
7 My teammates can be honest with me. They know I will be ______.	☐	☐	☐

Scoring: Give yourself 3 points for each *Always* answer, 1 point for each *Sometimes* answer, and no points for each *Never* answer.

15–21 points:	You're a great team player!
7–14 points:	Not bad, but you have room to grow.
0–6 points:	Think about how you can improve your teamwork skills.

Vocabulary practice 5

Exercise (A)

Complete the puzzle.

Across

5 a way of thinking about a situation, subject, or problem

6 a problem or subject that people are thinking and talking about

9 a statement saying that something is true (when it may not be)

10 seen by many people as good, important, and serious

12 to decide what something is or say who someone is

Down

1 things that show you that something is true or exists

2 the person, place, or group that a piece of information comes from

3 to study something carefully to understand it well

4 to describe someone who doesn't say the truth

7 to decide how good or important something is

8 choices you make after thinking about things

11 to go back and study something again to decide if it needs to change

Exercise (B)

Use 7 words from the puzzle to complete these notes from a talk about critical thinking.

CRITICAL THINKING = a set of skills you use to 1 ______________ information (examine the info carefully) so you can get a complete understanding of it

- *It helps you 2 ______________ the information (decide how good/true it is)*
- *It's important for making good 3 ______________, especially when you are basing them on information from people with different ideas about a subject*

Steps

1 Get info from more than one 4 ______________.
Try to understand each person's or group's 5 ______________: Why do they think that way?

2 Decide: What's fact and what's just opinion? How strong is the 6 ______________?

3 Make your own decision.

4 Take a 2nd look at how you made your decision—7 ______________ your steps.

Vocabulary practice 6

Exercise (A)

Read the clues and find the words.

A	G	R	I	S	K	I	F	A	D	M	I	T	R	E
L	A	E	X	P	O	M	O	T	I	V	A	T	E	N
Y	W	Q	U	A	L	I	T	Y	N	U	A	C	S	U
I	J	U	D	G	E	V	A	J	I	N	C	K	P	R
G	O	H	O	U	T	G	O	I	N	G	C	X	O	E
N	Z	S	M	N	H	L	R	A	N	V	E	Y	N	S
O	F	V	A	L	U	E	Y	D	O	A	P	M	S	P
R	E	D	P	O	S	I	T	I	V	E	T	Z	I	E
E	E	W	K	J	L	Y	U	B	A	K	E	A	B	C
O	D	L	R	W	A	T	T	I	T	U	D	E	I	T
I	B	R	A	V	E	Y	H	P	I	F	C	B	L	M
V	A	X	E	Z	D	G	E	S	O	Z	O	H	I	C
A	C	O	P	P	O	R	T	U	N	I	T	Y	T	Y
O	K	Y	L	T	V	A	L	Y	S	N	O	X	Y	A
N	R	U	W	H	A	B	I	N	S	P	I	R	E	Z

1 My manager gives me ______________ so that I know how well I'm doing.

2 My team works well together. We all have a good ______________ about teamwork.

3 You can show ______________ by listening to people with interest.

4 A new job would give me the ______________ to learn new skills.

5 Honesty is an important ______________ in a friend.

6 Everyone on the team shares ______________ for solving problems.

7 My company is a leader in the industry because of our many ______________.

8 Good pay is important to me, but other things ______________ me more.

9 Do any famous people ______________ you?

10 Please tell me what you think of my idea. I ______________ your opinion.

11 You have to be ______________ to try things you're afraid to do.

12 She's very nice, but she's usually quiet, not very ______________.

Exercise (B)

Use 6 words from the puzzle to complete Dan's email to the president of his company.

Email

Daniel Garcia
To: Helen Washington
Subject: Would you give me the 1 ______________ to interview you?

Dear Ms. Washington,

I'm studying business part-time at Northern University. For a class project, I need to interview a business leader.

Would you be able to give me 20 minutes of your time?

Here are some of the questions I'd like to ask you.

- What is the most important 2 ______________ for a leader to have?
- Which famous business leaders do you 3 ______________ the most?
- How do you 4 ______________ employees to work hard?
- You are well-respected in the industry for your 5 ______________, first as an engineer, now as a business leader. How do you think of so many new ideas?
- What is the hardest part of having so much 6 ______________?

I hope to speak with you soon. Thank you very much.

Vocabulary practice 7

Exercise (A)

Complete the puzzle.

Across

3 If you're working slowly, or not at all, but then you're able to get all your work done, you do this.

7 If you delay doing a task, then you do this to that task.

8 If you have a lot of work you must do, then you have a large or heavy this.

10 If you're able to keep things arranged in a carefully planned way, then this describes you.

12 If someone has told you to do a task, then they have given you this.

Down

1 If there's something that worries you a lot, then this word probably describes that thing.

2 If you have tasks that are like one another in some way, you can group them into these.

4 If something is too much for you to think about or deal with, then you are this.

5 If the things you need to do become so many that they're hard to manage, then they do this.

6 If you're using well-planned ways to reach a goal, then you're using these.

9 If there's a time or date by which you have to finish a task, then that time or date is this.

11 If you put tasks in order based on how important they are, you do this to them.

Exercise (B)

Use 8 words from the puzzle to complete the conversations.

1

My work just keeps piling up and piling up. I'm afraid I'll never 1 ______________!

You sound 2 ______________. Can you get some help?

2

You seem to be good at managing your time. What are your 3 ______________?

Let me show you the calendar I use. It really helps me stay 4 ______________.

3

One of my co-workers is sick, and I have to manage both my workload and his. It's very 5 ______________.

Can you 6 ______________ any of the work until he gets back?

4

The 7 ______________ for this project is Friday. Do you think we can finish by then?

I don't know. It's a difficult 8 ______________.

Vocabulary practice 8

Exercise (A)

Complete the puzzle. What is the vertical word?

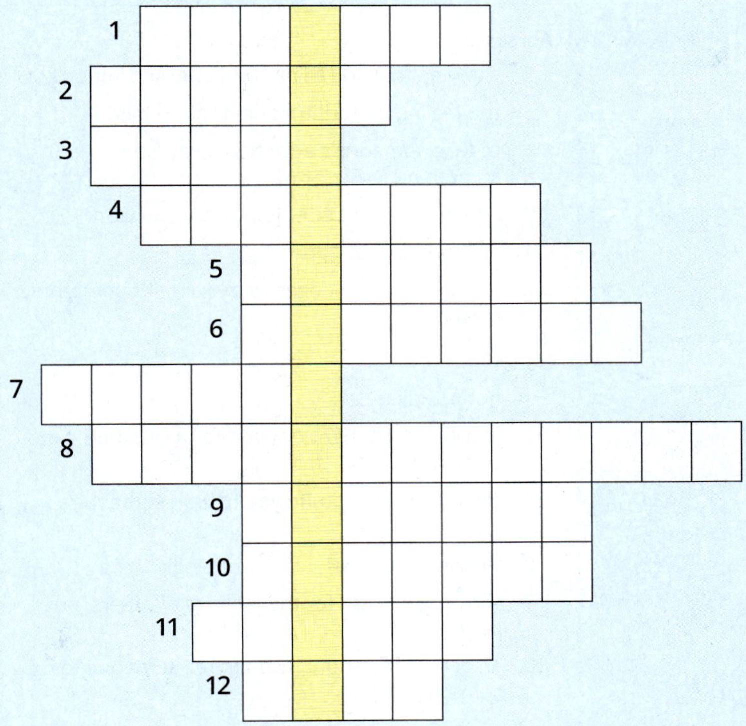

1 Parts inside your body that help you move: *the ________ of the arms and legs*

2 Relating to the human mind: *good ________ health*

3 Parts of plants we can eat but can't digest: *fruit that is high in ________*

4 A medical problem related to sugar in the blood: *get tested for ________*

5 Birds kept on farms to get meat and eggs from: *chicken and other kinds of ________*

6 Relating to the body rather than the mind or feelings: *in poor ________ health*

7 What can happen to a person's body in an accident: *see a doctor about an ________*

8 The force of blood moving through the human body: *the danger of high ________*

9 Something in foods like eggs and fish that helps your body grow: *foods full of ________*

10 A type of sugar that is in milk: *choose ________-free milk or yogurt*

11 Describing a person who moves a lot, doing different things: *a very ________ life*

12 Describing meat without much fat on it: *choose ________ meats*

Exercise (B)

Use 8 words from the puzzle to complete the questions and advice at a website on healthy habits.

STAYING HEALTHY

- Is there enough [1] ________ in your diet? Your body can get it from eating meat, fish, and [2] ________, for example.
- Are you eating too much fat? Try not to! Choose [3] ________ meats.
- Do you eat fresh fruit and vegetables every day? They will give you the [4] ________ your body needs.
- Do you enjoy milk and other dairy products? Some people avoid dairy products because of the [5] ________ in milk. But you can buy milk without it.
- Do you exercise every day? It's important to stay [6] ________. Getting enough exercise will build stronger [7] ________. It will also help you keep your [8] ________ low.

Vocabulary practice 9

Exercise (A)

Complete the puzzle.

Across

3 showing that you think someone isn't important
5 the feeling that a situation or place has
6 to take someone's attention away from something
7 a move up to a better job where you work
11 able to get a lot done
12 to make small changes to try to make something better

Down

1 not positive
2 in a way that's right or good for a situation, time, or place
4 the feeling or attitude you hear in someone's voice
8 to give all your attention to a single thing
9 showing no care for the feelings of others, not polite
10 an action or a sound used to tell someone to do something

Exercise (B)

Use 8 words from the puzzle to complete Chris's email to a friend.

Email

Chris London
To: Lee Jackson
Subject: My new job

Hi Lee,

Well, my first week at the new job is over, and I don't think I'm going to like it here. The 1 ____________ in the office isn't good. People aren't friendly.

I've been trying to 2 ____________ on my work. I want to be 3 ____________ and make a good impression, but I'm new, so I have many questions. I tried to ask the guy who sits next to me, but he said, "Look, I'm busy. Don't 4 ____________ me from my work." Then he turned his chair so his back was facing me. That was a clear 5 ____________ not to speak to him again!

Most of the others in the office aren't as 6 ____________ as that guy. Their words seem polite enough, but I can hear in their 7 ____________ of voice that they want me to go away.

I'm sorry I sound so 8 ____________ in this email, but it was a hard week and I'm not feeling very hopeful about this job. I'll tell you more when I see you tomorrow.

Vocabulary practice 10

Exercise (A)

Read the clues and find the words and phrases.

B	U	P	O	D	E	L	W	C	O	N	T	A	C	T
A	K	R	R	E	A	C	H	O	U	T	J	H	X	R
U	P	E	R	S	O	N	A	L	I	T	Y	Z	M	E
D	I	S	V	C	D	E	F	I	N	E	K	R	Y	V
I	Y	E	F	R	U	Y	P	G	M	R	L	E	F	N
E	H	N	G	I	Q	C	R	E	A	T	I	V	E	I
N	X	T	D	P	U	R	E	Z	C	J	W	I	M	M
C	E	M	A	T	C	H	F	O	H	N	O	S	P	P
E	O	C	N	I	P	Y	L	W	I	K	J	E	H	R
M	N	Y	X	O	B	R	E	H	E	S	Q	U	A	E
Z	G	R	A	N	A	X	C	B	V	Y	P	C	S	S
C	O	W	V	K	Q	V	T	F	E	X	W	G	I	S
V	I	H	I	G	H	L	I	G	H	T	L	O	Z	I
U	N	P	F	J	E	T	O	N	O	T	I	C	E	X
M	G	O	I	N	T	E	L	L	I	G	E	N	T	R

1 We haven't finished the planning. It's ______________.
2 My manager knows how to ______________ the right people to the right jobs.
3 Everyone likes her. She has a wonderful ______________.
4 Include your greatest strengths when you write a ______________ of yourself.
5 You have lots of great new ideas. You're such a ______________ person!
6 What's your goal? What do you want to ______________?
7 If you prepare well for your presentation, I'm sure you'll ______________ your boss.
8 The ways you spend your time and money ______________ your values. They show what's important to you.
9 If you never speak up and offer your ideas, people won't ______________ you.
10 The situation has changed, so we'll have to ______________ our plans.
11 Your cover letter gives you a chance to ______________ your strengths.
12 In the interview, remember to ______________ your best qualities.

Exercise (B)

Use 7 words from the puzzle to complete these notes from a talk on building your personal brand.

YOUR PERSONAL BRAND = your skills, experience, attitudes, and [1] ______________

Finding/building your brand–how to?

Ask yourself: What makes you different?
What makes people [2] ______________ you and remember you?

To Do:
1. Write a [3] ______________ of yourself. (Get ideas from family, friends, co-workers. Ask, "How would you describe me?")
2. Think about the future. What do I want to [4] ______________? Write down goals.
3. Decide who's the audience for my personal brand:
   - Who do I want to [5] ______________ with my skills and my strengths?
   - How do I [6] ______________ my good qualities to get the attention of those people?
4. Take another look at my résumé. Does it reflect me well, or do I need to [7] ______________ it?

Vocabulary practice 11

Exercise (A)

Complete the puzzle.

Across

1 If you have friends that don't like each other, you probably go out with them this way.

7 If your networking produces good results, then you can describe it like this.

10 If you keep in contact with someone (by email, for example), then you stay like this with them.

11 If you add people to your network so it's larger, then you do this to it.

12 If you try to contact someone, then you do this.

Down

2 If you share the same interests as someone, the two of you might do this well.

3 If you plan a small informal meeting with friends, then you'll have this.

4 If you get a relationship started, then you do this to it.

5 If you need help to decide what to do, then ask friends for this.

6 If you let your network know what you're doing now, then they're getting this from you.

8 If you need to learn how to do a job, then you need this.

9 If you are doing something to reach a goal, then you have this.

Exercise (B)

Use 8 words from the puzzle to complete the conversations.

1

How was the 1 ____________? Did you learn anything?

Yes, I learned a LOT! I thought it was very 2 ____________.

2

I'm planning a little 3 ____________ with people from my last job. Want to come?

Thanks! I'd like to meet them. I'm trying to 4 ____________ my network.

3

When is Anna coming back to work? Have you had a recent 5 ____________ from her?

She sent pictures of the baby a couple of weeks ago. I'll 6 ____________ to her today.

4

Have you stayed 7 ____________ any of your professors from the university?

Just two of them. I call them to ask for 8 ____________ sometimes.

Vocabulary practice 12

Exercise A

Complete the puzzle. What is the vertical word?

1 There were several ____________ for the job who had excellent skills.
2 When you apply for a job, they'll ask you for the names of ____________.
3 Be ready to explain at your interview why you're ____________ for the job.
4 Wearing the right clothes to an interview helps you feel comfortable and ____________.
5 We need to write a job description that lists all the ____________ for the job.
6 "Business ____________" is a style of clothing that is less formal than a suit.
7 At my company, we all wear jeans to work. There is no formal ____________.
8 If you get the job, what will you have to do? What will your ____________ be?
9 You should read this online ____________ of people's experiences in job interviews.
10 How will you organize all the letters and other ____________ related to your job search?
11 The clothes you wear to work should always be ____________ and clean.
12 You won't want to work at the company if you don't agree with their ____________.

Exercise B

Use 8 words from the puzzle to complete Dana's email to a friend.

Email

Dana Kennedy
To: Jia Reed
Subject: Work

Hey Jia,

I just heard about a new job opening at work! It would be a big step up for me, but I think I'd be 1 ____________ for the job. I saw the job description, so I know what they're looking for. I can meet all the 2 ____________ for the job. I'm 3 ____________ that my communication skills are strong enough.

But I know there will be a lot of other 4 ____________. Maybe the fact that I already work here will help. I've had a 5 ____________ about the position with my manager, and she says I should go for it.

I do worry that some people here will think I'm too young. Maybe I should try to look older and more 6 ____________ in the way I dress. In this office, we don't have a 7 ____________, so I usually just wear 8 ____________ clothes, like jeans and T-shirts. Maybe I should dress for the job I *want* instead of the job I *have*.

GLOSSARY

Glossary

Module 1: Communication 1

design (n) a drawing of something new that will be made
designer (n) someone whose job is to make plans or patterns for clothes, furniture, equipment, etc.
negatively (adv) in a way that shows dislike of something
software (n) a set of programs that tells a computer to do something
specialist (n) someone who knows a lot about a subject, or is skilled at doing something

Module 2: Communication 2

annoying (adj) something that makes you feel a little angry
bored (adj) if you are bored, you feel that what you are doing, watching, or hearing is not interesting
cough (v) if you cough, air suddenly comes out of your throat with a short rough sound
habit (n) something that you do often or regularly
sneeze (v) to make air suddenly come out of your nose and mouth, for example, because you have a cold

Module 3: Goal Setting

achieve (v) to succeed in doing or getting something you want
keep your resolution (phr) to do what you have promised to do

Module 4: Teamwork

cleanup (n) a process in which you get rid of dirt or waste from a place
donate (v) to give something useful to a person or an organization that needs help
event (n) something that has been organised, such as a party, sports game, or show
gardening (n) the work of growing plants in a garden
volunteer (n) someone who does something to help other people without being paid

Module 5: Critical Thinking

chain (n) a number of stores, hotels, or other businesses owned by the same person or company
council (n) a group of people who have been chosen to make laws for a town or organisation
graduate (n) someone who has finished studying at school, college, or university and has a diploma or a degree
lane (n) one of the parts that a wide road is divided into, so that people can drive along next to each other
recent (adj) happening or done a short time ago
sidewalk (n) a path with a hard surface, that you walk on next to a street

Module 6: Leadership

cabinet (n) a piece of furniture with shelves covered by a door or drawer
climate (n) the type of weather that a place usually has
environmentalist (n) someone who is concerned about protecting the environment
make sure (phr) to ensure that something is done or that it happens
protest (v) if a group of people protest, they show in public that they do not agree with something
protest (n) a public event where a large group of people show that they do not agree with something
receptionist (n) someone whose job is to answer the phone and welcome people when they arrive at an office or hotel
run out (phr v) to use all of something, so that there is none left

Module 7: Self-Management

advertisement (n) a picture or short movie which tries to make people buy a product or use a service
caterer (n) person or company that is paid to provide and serve food and drinks at a party, meeting, etc.
hire (v) to pay someone to work for you
in advance (phr) ahead of time
juggle (v) to try to do two or more jobs or activities at the same time
lighting (n) the lights in a building or street, or how bright the lights are
paperwork (n) official pieces of paper that you must write information on in order to do something or get something
plumbing (n) the system of water pipes in a building

Module 8: Wellness

fitness (n) the condition of being healthy and strong
keep track of (phr) to make sure you have the information you need
slice (n) a flat piece of bread, meat, or pie that is cut from a whole
trigger (n) a thing that makes something start to happen

Module 9: Social Responsibility

connected (adj) if two or more things are connected, there is some kind of relationship between them
pharmacy (n) a store that sells medicines
regular (adj) happening or repeated at the same time every second, hour, day, etc.
snack (n) something that you eat between meals

Glossary

Module 10: Branding

animation* (n) the process of making movies with drawings or models, rather than filming actors
degree* (n) an official statement that says you have successfully completed all your studies at a university or college
internship* (n) a job that lasts for a short time, which someone does in order to gain experience
job applicant (n) person who applies for a job
patient (n) someone receiving medical treatment from a doctor or in a hospital
patient (adj) able to deal with a problem or wait for something without getting angry or upset

* in audio

Module 11: Job Search

attend (v) to be at a meeting, class, or special event
lecture (n) a formal talk to a group of people about a subject
pharmacy (n) the study or practice of preparing drugs and medicine

Module 12: Interviewing

accompany (v) to go somewhere with someone
construction (n) something that has been built

Notes